Teenager Trouble-shooting:
How to Stop Your Adolescent Driving You Crazy

By

Dr Darryl Cross

By the same Author:
"Growing up Children: How To Get 5 – 12 Year Olds To Behave & Do As They're Told"

First edition published in Australia 2003
This new edition published 2009
Cover design by LuminousEye

Booksurge Publishing

ISBN: 1-4196-9749-8
ISBN-13: 978-1-4196-9749-4

Visit www.booksurge.com to order additional copies

Testimonials

"It's a must read for parents of teenagers. It is full of insights and practical suggestions to help you survive those tumultuous years."

Dr Terri Ano, Managing Director,
Pegasus Partners, Washington, USA

"Thank you Darryl for a book that has been my ray of hope when I have felt at a loss of knowing the best way to handle various situations I have had to confront with my teenage daughter.

Your book is written in such conversational sound and practical language it is like I am receiving great insight whilst sitting down having a coffee.

It is a book that I keep coming back to as the need arises and would strongly encourage any parent of a teenager to get hold of it whether that teenager presents as challenging or not."

Jacqui Banham, Consultant,
Stirling, South Australia, Australia

"Dr Cross has created a distinctly practical and reassuring book that parents will benefit from immensely. The book includes a wealth of suggestions, ideas and specific actions that may need to be taken by parents to help them better understand situations from the teenager's perspective and respond to them.

Parents of teenagers will appreciate not only the real-life stories and their explanations, but practitioners too would be wise to absorb the thinking and approach that has been adopted, because the book is a lesson in clarity, simplicity of writing style and contains some humor too.

This book is a masterclass on teenage issues and hence parents and therapists should have a copy to hand and refer to it whenever the need arises."
Geoff Carter, Business Success Consultant, Killorglin, County Kerry, Ireland

"There are plenty of times that you feel inadequate as a parent of a teenager and there are not many places that you can turn to for help and advice.

Dr Darryl Cross' book, "Teenager Trouble-Shooting" is one such place. It offers lots of helpful hints about parenting adolescents and they're presented in a very readable way. Although you can easily read this book from cover to cover, it's set out in such a way that it's easy to find guidance on specific issues.

Dr Cross has distilled his reading and his professional experience into one easy-to-follow instruction manual for all parents. There's even a Frequently Asked Questions chapter!"
Viano Jaksa, Chairman, St Paul's College Board, South Australia, Australia

"Being second time around parents...I marvel at the question – how did our first two survive the growing up of their parents? Darryl's communicative style will have first time parents finding comfort and direction as they try out their un-tested parenting skills, and not so new parents nodding their head in agreement as they relate from past experiences. Thank you Darryl for supporting parents in such a critical life function, raising our children, that we so often must learn by trial and error."
Richard B. Kendall, Principal, Gordon, Hughes & Banks, LLP, Business Advisory Services, Golden, Colorado, USA

"In this book Darryl details for us the essential issues of adolescence and the incredible experience for the teenager, the parents and the whole family….Identity with independence, but connection, what a great formula for living.

I recommend this book to all families that want to look at these crucial issues.   It is an informative text, but elaborated in a warm and very human way."

John G. McManus, Chief Psychologist, Corporate Health Services, Sydney, New South Wales, Australia

"This is the kind of book that school principals would wish that many of their parents would read and act on…it contains a wealth of practical experience about how to manage adolescents.....there is nothing theoretical about this book....and it covers nitty-gritty areas that parents often ask about.

I wish this book had been around years ago."

Chris McCabe, Principal, Xavier College, Victoria, Melbourne, Australia

"My children are now in their 20's – I wish I'd had this book 10 years ago!   Clear, concise and comforting strategies to help parents and teens through both the difficult and rewarding years."

Noel Guilford, Business Consultant, Guilford Consulting, Balderton, Chester, Cheshire, United Kingdom

"This book is in effect a coaching manual for parents….The pointers provided to effective parenting represent much more than a "pep talk." The reader is specifically shown how to develop their parenting skills in a way that will enhance both their self-efficacy and self-esteem.

I strongly recommend this book for parents of adolescents. It also is a useful resource for others with a duty of care for young people in this age group."
Professor John Taplin, Pro-Vice Chancellor, University of Adelaide, South Australia, Australia

"An excellent aid for parents raising teenagers. It provides understanding and practical tips which if followed will guide you through the many challenges. An important book for parents who care."
Peter Marshman, Chairman, Youth Opportunities Inc, Somerton Park, South Australia, Australia

"A fascinating read. We have a blended family, with three teenage boys (16, 18, 19) from two earlier marriages. One is now with us, one at college in the US and one in the UK....there are many invaluable strategies in your books -- not just for dealing with problems, which is where much literature focuses, but for giving direction. Thanks."
Andrew Thoseby, Director, 1st Executive Pty Ltd, Melbourne, Victoria, Australia

"What an amazing piece of wisdom, shared in a manner you would liken to a good friend chatting over a "cuppa". Your work in this book is so inviting, I had to keep reading, I couldn't put it down to pick up tomorrow.
There were numerous examples of, "I can relate to that," and several instances of, "Wow! I'm glad I found out about that." I loved the comic style illustrations, the clear diagrams, the meaningful small quotes, and particularly the "real life" examples in grey boxes.
To me, this book is a great conversation with a trusted friend about my children.

Thank you for writing it and sharing it with myself and others. I am very fortunate to have been able to read 'Teenager Trouble-Shooting,' and one day I'm sure my son and daughter will appreciate the fact that I read it too."

Peter Kostiw, Principal, Catholic Education, West Lakes, South Australia, Australia

FOREWORD

When growing up, in many societies, the transition is from childhood to adulthood via some form of rite de passage. In our society, as Dr Cross points out, this ceremony has been lost and there is a period of dalliance between childhood and maturity when young persons are not quite sure of their status. They have to work their way through a confusing pattern of events full of ambiguity. In one breath, they are told that they are mature and to act their age, and in the other, that they are not old enough to make certain decisions. One expert described adolescence as a period when young persons are not quite children, not quite adults, and not quite sure of themselves. They are mature enough to leave school at 15 years, drive a car at 17 years and see an R-rated movie at 18 years. But when are they adults?

The expertise of Dr Cross, a lecturer, coach, counselor and psychologist shines through in his written work. This book is so easy to read. All of the underlying theories of adolescence are there, but without the esoteric academic jargon of the professional. Dr Cross has simplified the theory which is what makes the book easily readable and understandable. The analogy of building a house with its early foundations in childhood, walls during adolescence, and roof during adulthood is an example of how he can condense developmental principles into a concrete model to help elucidate the message that he is espousing.

Although Dr Cross expresses it slightly differently from the way I have in the past, his chapter on identity is vital for parents and guardians to understand if they are going to understand their adolescents. There are three central questions in the adolescent's search for identity: Who am I? Where am I going? And What am I going to do when I get there? In this journey, they have to cope with physical, sexual, cognitive, and other maturational changes and attendant social, emotional, moral, economic and vocational consequences. Here, they have to achieve a balance between youthful idealism and economic realism.

Adolescents need recognition, as Dr Cross so adequately points out. They need help and support in finding their talents and in enriching them. As importantly as at any other time of our lives, we need success and the éclat that comes with it. Although we readily recognize the aphorism, "Nothing succeeds like success," certainly during adolescence, the obverse is true, "Nothing fails like failure." If adolescents do not achieve recognition for some talent they possess, they make seek their recognition in inappropriate ways by acting out, promiscuity, becoming the class clown, the delinquent, the bully, or the drug addict. To them it is better to be one of these notorious people that to be a nobody with no stimulus value.

Children are given vaccines to immunize them from the perils of disease. On the road to adulthood, there are many challenges and choices to make, that lead us to one path or another. Unfortunately, in our busy world, some of these choices can lead the young person to the perils of society: drug use, vandalism, inappropriate sexual activity, truancy, shoplifting or delinquency. Dr Cross counsels parents to listen and to talk to their adolescents, just not to expect that at a certain age, they will be mature and everything will be alright. Children should be taught to be independent over a period of time. The guidelines, signposts, and beacons that they are given allow them to gradually become more independent as they are released over time. This is called behavioral immunization.

This book is full of serious case studies to illustrate the points that Dr Cross is making, but it has its humorous side as well, with so many truisms illustrated in the cartoons scattered throughout its scholarly pages.

Don't just read this book and put it on your library shelf. It is a book that you should read and re-read. In each re-reading, you will pick up new insights, hints and tips to help you cope with, and know, your adolescent child in greater depth. And another thing, although Dr Cross has written this book for parents, we should keep in mind the words of Dr Arthur Jersild, an American expert, who claimed that those who can profit most from a study of adolescence, are the adolescents themselves. I recommend that parents give it to the adolescent children to read as well, since there are many insights that may help them in their journey as they search for their identity.

Emeritus Professor John K Collins
Department of Psychology
Macquarie University
New South Wales
Australia

CONTENTS

CONTENTS Continued

Disclaimer

CHAPTER 1

What Happened to the Training Manual?

Who said parenting was easy?

Being a parent can be downright difficult. It can bring men who are strong and dominating in their sports, their businesses or work-places to their knees. It can bring women who are bright, capable, well-organized and outgoing to be miserable and downcast.

Parenting is certainly a challenge. It also brings great reward.

"There's only one pretty child in the world, and every mother has it."

(Proverb)

I have heard so many stories in which a couple was so keen to have a child that they could love, care for and enjoy. Then along comes gorgeous little Michelle or

Michael. This is the baby that they wanted. This is the baby that they longed for.

However, before long, their dreams start falling apart. Gone is the peace and harmony, the family routine, structure and organization.

Instead, there is stress and tension, constant disharmony and fighting. The child and the parents are out of control. This is the baby that at times the parents would gladly give away. The dream has turned into a nightmare. Then comes adolescence. If they thought that the early years were hard, wait until adolescence hits!

The jewel in the crown has turned into the stone in the ground!

Peter and Louise rang my consulting rooms to make an urgent appointment saying that they were thoroughly frustrated and needed to see someone straight away. They explained to my secretary that they had all but given up hope in managing their 15-year-old daughter Sarah. They had had difficulties managing her for some years, and now the school had suspended her for disruptive behaviour. They were mortified that this had occurred.

Sarah was clearly not happy to be in my waiting room with her parents. She slunk down in the chair, looked down at the floor and appeared angry and listened to her iPod with her ear-phones.

In my office, she sat turned away from her parents. Mom and dad gave a brief explanation as to what had brought them all there. Sarah said nothing. As quickly as possible, I ushered the parents out. They seemed to be caring parents, but remaining in my office was not helping the situation.

"Sarah" I said, "I gather it wasn't your idea to come today...in fact, it looks like you were dragged along by your parents...and I can expect that you can probably think of a thousand things that you'd rather be doing than talking to a dude like me." She looked up and there was a faint recognition.

I went on, "There's nothing Sarah that says you have to stay and talk to me. I know that mum and dad have brought you here, but I'm not here to make your life a misery. You don't have to talk to me. If you want to talk to me, I'd be glad to talk to you, but if you don't want to, that's ok because I'm sure that your parents will take up the consulting time to chat with me. What would you like to do? It's your choice."

Sarah stayed to talk. Beneath the hurt and angry exterior was really a heartfelt young woman and a confused young woman. She admitted to being lost. She certainly resented her parents, but she was willing to talk and she did so for a number of sessions.

Sarah eventually started to confide more in her mother and her behavior settled somewhat. Over her adolescent years, there was the occasional aberration at which time she would come in to see me for a couple more sessions.

She finally graduated from high school and went into a hospitality course.

Adolescence is a confusing time for most – in a real

sense, it's uncharted waters for the teenager as well as
for the parents.

And when we all get through it, it is triumph indeed.

No training courses

It seems incredible to me, that there really is a
complete lack of training in our community on how to be
parents.

It seems incredible that the two most basic and
important roles that sustain and underpin our whole
community, that of being a marriage or permanent
partner, and that of being a parent, involve **no real
training or instruction** at all.

---

*"Being an effective partner and parent are
two important roles that underpin the fabric
of our society – so how is it that we don't
receive any training in either?"*

(Darryl Cross)

Certainly, there are some organizations, particularly
those that are church related, that do offer pre-marriage
courses and that do offer short parenting courses. But
generally speaking, while these are well-intentioned, they
are only short courses and cannot be expected to bring
about effective change in peoples' attitudes and behavior.

Typically too, the people who attend these kinds of

courses are usually the "converted" who are probably reasonably effective in their communication and interactions anyway, and in their general ability to be parents. It's the same old story. Those who really do need such courses generally do not access them.

It is interesting to ask the question that if the continuance of our society depends on appropriate parenting and rearing of our children, how come we're leaving it to chance somehow?

Where are the intensive courses which will allow us to feel confident in our role of parenting? What are we doing to counteract a dilemma that is permeating the community – namely, parents who don't know how to be parents and yet have nowhere to turn to learn the necessary skills?

If you answered that there are government agencies available, then you would be right, but a closer look would tell you that these are understaffed and under resourced.

"How is it that almost all of us have had more training in learning to drive a car than we have had in learning to be a parent?"

(Darryl Cross)

If you answered that there are welfare and church organizations available, then you would be right, but a closer look would also tell you that these are hopelessly under-financed.

No training manuals

Recently, when I bought a new washing machine, there was a comprehensive manual that told me everything I needed to know about the appliance. It even had a section at the rear of the booklet titled "troubleshooting" which has been invaluable on a few occasions.

In fact, as I write, I just purchased a digital camera and needless to say, it has come with a very well illustrated "Owner's Manual" with photos and diagrams and a clear explanation. There are particular sections devoted to specific problems that the user could encounter over time.

When each of my three children were born however, there was no such training manual and no guidelines.

The tragedy is that you and I have had more training in how to drive a car, work a computer, use a piece of software or use a mobile phone than we have had in being a parent.

I remember vividly when I first walked down the hospital steps with our first born in a bassinet and placed him in the back seat of the car to take him home. I remember feeling overcome with a general sensation, "What do we do now?" There was no training manual. There was no comprehensive booklet. There was no section entitled "trouble-shooting". There was no nurse, teacher, trainer, coach or mentor. There was no-one. Just us and this baby. And the baby was so little and so, so dependent on us. This was not exactly how I imagined it.

"Never have children, only grandchildren."

(Gore Vidal; 1925-, USA Novelist)

While this book you are reading is not strictly a manual, it is indeed a recipe book of ideas and techniques that you might find valuable.

Needless to say, the recipes are tried-and-true over three decades of working as a psychologist, of having worked in a clinical hospital setting, as well as in my own private psychology practice, and having raised three wonderful children who are now young adults.

I sincerely trust that this book will give you the tools to be more effective parents and give you greater confidence in your parenting of adolescents.

CHAPTER 1 SUMMARY

Who said parenting was easy?

Being a parent can be downright difficult. It is one of the most difficult jobs, but it is also one of the most rewarding.

No training courses

It seems incredible that the two most basic and important roles that sustain and underpin our whole community, that of being a marriage or permanent partner, and that of being a parent, involve **no** real training or instruction at all.

It is interesting to ask the question that if the continuance of our society depends on appropriate parenting and rearing of our children, how come we're leaving it to chance somehow?

No training manuals

We have training manuals for our computers, our new technology, our kitchen appliances, our televisions and so on. Where is the one about dealing with teenagers?

This book seeks to provide those answers.

CHAPTER 2

Some Basics of Life

It's a familiar tale. As parents we feel helpless at times. We run out of ideas; of things to do; of ways to approach a situation. We also run out of patience. Why can't they (the adolescent) just do as they're told? Why do they always have to push the limits?

Nigel's parents sat in front of me in the office really at their "wits end" and despairing about what they could do. They said that Nigel was an only child who had been essentially a well-behaved boy as far as his parents were concerned until 9th Grade (Year 9) when he was 14 years of age.

Apparently suddenly, he had given up on his studies; he was not completing homework, and he was getting into trouble at school. After school each afternoon, he was going with a specific group of boys who had a reputation for anti-social behavior such as vandalism, graffiti, and there was a rumor around the school that these boys were also into drug taking. Nigel was now refusing to do as his parents asked and when they stipulated that he was not to go out each afternoon with his peer group, he told them that they couldn't stop him and anyway, it was his life.

These parents were desperate for help. "What can we do?" they said, "Where did we go wrong?" "Where will he end up?" "Is he into drugs?" "How can we get through to him?"

It is true to say that life is often full of paradoxes or apparent contradictions. Nowhere is this more obvious than in adolescence.

With adolescence, there are the ups and the downs, kind of like a roller coaster ride or being on a see-saw (except a see-saw is a bit more predictable than a roller coaster ride or an adolescent!). It is not surprising therefore that in this respect, there are some facts that need to be understood in this whole discussion of adolescence.

1. The critical years

Although adolescence is the topic of this book, we need to understand that *the critical years for child rearing are really between about 0 to 7 years*.

Irrespective of which childhood development book you might read, the message is the same, the early years are the ones when the basic personality is laid down and developed.

The implication is that if you haven't managed as a parent to get it more or less right in those early formative years, the chances of getting it "right" in the adolescent years are diminished.

However, don't give up hope.

The old saying of "better late than never" is definitely true. Still, if the horse has bolted as the saying goes, it just makes it that much harder to rein in later.

I am reminded of the Jesuit adage which states, "Give me a child until he is 7, and I'll show you the [person]."

"The first 7 years for a child hold the key – if you haven't got it more or less right by then as a parent, the horse may well have bolted."

(Darryl Cross)

It is those early years that are most important when you are teaching your children basic principles and values and showing them how to create good habits for living.

For example, tasks such as cleaning up after they have finished playing, making their bed each morning, and saying "please" or "thank you" are all basic habits that need to be laid down early.

You are teaching them to create good routines for living such as being organized to get off to school in the morning, doing homework before the television or computer gets turned on in the late afternoon. While you are teaching these things, the parent-child relationship is developing.

You've certainly heard the saying that a "leopard can't change its spots." The message is that it is in these younger years that you teach your children the "spots," the principles, the rules and values for living.

I recall the mother and father who lamented to me that now at 15 years of age, they wanted their daughter to make her bed and clean up her room. A good idea, but 10 years too late. In their desire to do their best for their daughter, these parents had cleaned up after her for all of her life. In the end, they had made a burden for themselves and prevented their daughter from learning early, a basic rule in life that has to do with being organized, looking after possessions, taking responsibility and cleaning up.

So even if in these early years we have struggled with our parenting and have not been proud of our efforts, it is important to decide to do it differently. Parenting and our impact on our children and adolescents can be changed. Human behaviour is such that our responses and reactions can be monitored and altered so that those around us, in turn, change accordingly.

**The early years are the formative years –
don't waste them.**

Life goes on

It is now a well-accepted principle that life is a series of stages that we grow through and each stage builds upon the previous stage.

However, what we perhaps didn't know and need to recognize is that even if we don't get the previous stage right, *life or growth goes on regardless,* but there may patches, cracks or gaps in our development. This notion was originally proposed by Sigmund Freud who borrowed the idea from embryologists. These experts tell us that there is an appointed time for all things.

If, for example, a limb does not form in the embryo at the correct or appointed time, human development goes on regardless and the human foetus will grow without that particular part and the baby has a deformity.

Freud, along with others since, has indicated that in similar ways, there are **stages of emotional growth**. If we do not learn the lessons of a particular stage, emotional growth goes on irrespectively, and later, we have somehow to deal with the gaps in our development.

Here is an example:

A wife asks for counseling, complaining about her husband whom she feels is irresponsible, unreliable and disorganized. She might even go so far as to say that he is selfish, lazy or "good for nothing."

Ask her to give some more detail and she replies that her husband leaves his clothes lying around, he is generally untidy, watches TV most of the time, won't help with household chores, won't do the necessary maintenance jobs around the home, is frequently away from the home watching or playing sport or some other hobby or interest, and certainly won't help with the children.

When you put to her the suggestion that her husband sounds just like a child, she readily agrees. She might well say, "Yes that's right, instead of having 2 kids, it's like I've got 3 kids!"

If as a counselor, you were tempted to ask about her husband's family, you may well find out that in his family where he grew up, the son was a bit like the father where mother was virtually the "slave" and picked up after the father just like she picked up after the son, and certainly did not demand that the son help around the house or do any chores. She probably reasoned that it was simply easier to do it herself and it simply wasn't worth the fuss or an argument.

So, the son never really progresses into adolescence and instead, although his mother is well intentioned, her son becomes stuck as a child.

What does this mean when he becomes an adult? How does he cope? He never successfully completed a specific stage of emotional growth and yet here he is as an adult. What does he unconsciously do? He ends up marrying another "mom!"

Here is another example:

Grant seeks counseling for his marriage. He is distressed, confused and at a loss to know what to do. He explains that he has been married a little over 7 years. He married when he was 30 and had worked hard to set himself up in a comfortable lifestyle with a car and apartment which he had virtually paid off.

He stated that during his marriage, he felt that he had done all he could to make his wife, Maria, happy and content. He had worked hard to try to establish them financially. He had tried to do the right thing around the home by helping out knowing that Maria worked too and that housework for example, needed to be shared. He cooked most meals. They took it in turns to do the shopping although she complained that it didn't fit in with her schedule. He had tried to be accommodating with her parents and friends and believed that he had been open to his wife's family and acquaintances.

Grant said that whatever he did never seemed to be good enough.

The car they drove wasn't the best in the street and his wife often remarked at other makes and models in their area and as they drove around. He said that Maria wanted the best townhouse in the best suburb and that they had mortgaged themselves heavily. She wanted the best of everything including furniture, house fittings, electrical goods and white-goods. She insisted that once a year they go on an overseas holiday even if it was just offshore such as the Great Barrier Reef. Of course, she had to have the designer label clothes too.

Grant said that he was now tired and fatigued and felt depressed about the money they owed. He couldn't keep up financially. He just couldn't seem to please her no matter what he did. He felt like giving up. He just couldn't go on like this. He became quite teary in the counseling session.

Our counseling session moved around to Maria's family and her parents.

What might you expect to find?

Grant explained that his wife's parents seemed nice, but on reflection, he felt that the father-in-law was a somewhat quiet man who kept largely to himself and seemed to be at the beck and call of his wife. He kept largely in the background. The mother was the dominating partner; he said that, "she seemed to wear the pants." The father-in-law rarely offered an opinion and largely agreed with his wife. Whatever the mother-in-law wanted, she got.

Their only child, Maria, seemed spoilt or at least, that's certainly what Grant had heard from various members of the extended family. In fact, at their wedding, Grant remembers an uncle and aunt saying in jest that they hoped that he could keep up with his new wife, Maria, and her demands.

So, inevitably, Maria marries her "father" whom she unconsciously expects will give her everything that she wants. I mean to say, Grant was well-heeled when they first met so why wouldn't he be able to fulfill her demands! Maria becomes stuck emotionally and never learns the lesson of independence and money management!

In this case, Grant reads that the marriage is in trouble and seeks help.

But what are the chances of this marriage being salvaged?

So, what does this all mean for adolescence?

Adolescence is all about:
- learning how to be independent and self-sufficient,
- learning how to make and keep relationships (same-sex and opposite sex),
- learning what it means to work and focus on a career direction.

If these lessons are not learned in adolescence, the individual continues in life, *but their development is short-circuited*.

There is certainly that percentage who never seem to grow up and somehow or other never seem to be able to make it through adolescence. They get stuck. **They just end up being big boys or girls, but with child-like attitudes and behavior.** Big boys and girls on the outside, but little girls and boys on the inside.The challenge for us as parents is to ensure that the full lessons of adolescence are learned for our children. No short-circuits.

Growing up is a bit like building a house

The diagram below depicts the various stages of growing up. There is a sense in which we can apply this house analogy to our own lives.

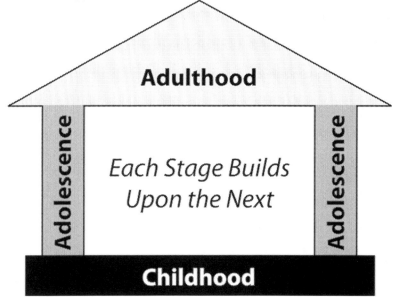

First, **the foundation** is laid. This occurs over about the **first seven years of life**. We cannot afford to take shortcuts with the foundation. It needs to be strong and well built because the rest of the house will rest on these foundations.

Of course, there may be small blemishes in the concrete which makes up the foundation, but what we want to guard against are the major cracks or faults that seriously weaken the foundation. These major faults occur with violence (physical and emotional) in the family, alcohol and drug abuse, chaos and craziness in the extreme, and abandonment of the child.

Secondly, up go **the walls**. This could be likened to the **period of adolescence**. If we follow this analogy through, if the foundation (or relationship) is strong, then we have a good basis on which to build the walls and the upright structures. If the foundations are badly flawed somehow, then as a consequence, we can expect the walls will develop cracks and problems.

This book however, is about supporting the walls in order to achieve the tasks of adolescence as previously mentioned above.

Finally, the **superstructure or roof** is added. This period could be likened to **adulthood**. Again, if the analogy holds true, providing we have done a good job with the foundation and then the walls, the ceiling and roof will not incur the kind of problems that might be experienced had we had difficulties with the foundation and walls. We can expect a solid and tight roof, if indeed, the foundation and walls have been well put together.

Life deals up all sorts of weather. Sometimes we

have pleasant days and at other times, the storms come including lightning, rain, hail and snow.

If our house is not strong and has cracks in the walls or gaps in the roof, then we are not as able to withstand the storms of life as we would if the foundations were strong, our walls well built and our superstructure and roof tight.

In other words, if because of our foundations, we are more tense and anxious than most, then our tolerance for stress is reduced, we feel more vulnerable, we find it difficult to cope, do not take as many risks and perhaps have more illnesses or days off sick.

[Regardless of our past though, we ought not to despair. There is always hope. We can change. In fact, I have also written a manual titled, *"How to Stop Your Self-Sabotage: Steps to Increase Your Self-Confidence"* which can be downloaded from my website at **www.drdarryl.com** . Our past does not have to predict our future. Put another way, you do not have to be your past.]

Children are all different

One important notion to understand is that the way you treat one child doesn't mean that you can treat another one the same way. Children are all different. As a Sunday School teacher once said to our class, "When God made each of you, He threw away the mould." Each child is unique.

Some parents ask, "How can it be that with the same biological parents that our kids can turn out so differently?" Other parents say, "Our two kids are like chalk and cheese, how come?" All children arrive on the planet with their own unique personalities.

Some are outgoing and extraverted; some are more inward looking and introverted. Some are placid and easy-going, others are difficult and temperamental. Some "hit the ground running" while others are content to just be. They just arrived that way.

My firstborn son is more introverted, introspective and thoughtful while the second son is the outgoing, party animal. The firstborn is more artistic and creative in nature while the second son is more into facts, details and logic. My daughter falls somewhere in between these two.

Children arrive as their own persons and then, the environment needs to help them develop as individuals.

My task as a father is to reinforce who they are as individuals and support their persons. For the firstborn, we encouraged his creative pursuits through writing; he is now a journalist. The second son could have gone into science or the humanities, but has now chosen to study the basics of argument and discerning fact from fantasy through a law degree. My daughter is headed towards public relations and is currently an event planner.

For children who are more active, physical and "busy," we need to ensure that we can satisfy who they are as persons by encouraging such activities as sports (e.g. football, netball, tennis etc) including water-sports such as water-skiing, surf-boarding or body-boarding.

For children who are always playing with Lego or making things, we need to encourage them to join the local model car racing club or perhaps the model airplane club or even the model boat club.

For the artistic boys and girls, we need to consider extra art classes, computer graphics, story writing, dancing or drama.

For the more difficult children who are often **the thrill-seekers and who take risks**, we need to sign them up for the local go-kart racing club, mountain bike club, down-hill bicycle club, motor-cross club, skate board club or even a stint at parachuting.

If we don't constructively channel their particular personalities, then we run the risk of them finding their own destructive "channels" which can often mean some activity outside of the law.

Our challenge as parents is to watch and observe our children's strengths, whatever they may be. Our next step is to decide how to build on those strengths and how to allow our children to make the most of their abilities and talents.

Without pushing or nagging, we allow our children the opportunity to test themselves in any number of arenas as they explore and extend their own assets and gifts.

"If I had to choose for my children between a smart intellect and a healthy self-esteem, I'd choose the latter every time."

(Darryl Cross)

CHAPTER 2 SUMMARY

The critical years

The early years are the important years. It is in those early years that you are teaching your child basic principles and values and showing them how to create good habits for living. These are the years when the basic personality is laid down.

Life goes on

It is now a well-accepted principle that life is a series of stages we grow through and each stage builds upon the previous stage.

If the lessons of adolescence are not learned, the individual continues in life, but their development is short-circuited.

Our job as parents is to ensure that there are no short-circuits.

There is certainly that percentage who never seem to grow up and somehow or other never seem to be able to make it through adolescence. They just end up being big boys or girls, but with child-like attitudes and behavior.

Growing up is a bit like building a house

First, the foundations are laid, and this is our childhood. Next comes the walls, and this is our adolescence. Finally, there is the roof, and this is our adulthood.

Life deals up all sorts of weather. If our house is not strong and has cracks in the walls or gaps in the roof, then we are not as able to withstand the storms of life as we would if the foundations were strong, our walls well built and our superstructure and roof tight.

Children are all different

One important notion to understand is that the way you treat one child doesn't mean that you can treat another one the same way. Children are all different.

All children arrive on the planet with their own unique personalities.

Our challenge as parents is to watch and observe our children's strengths, whatever they may be.

Our next step is to decide how to build on those strengths and how to allow our children to make the most of their abilities and talents.

CHAPTER 3

Independence:
The Task of Parents & Adolescents

Independence

There are **two** stages in life when you can expect parenting to be "rocky". Both have to do with *gaining independence*. What are they?

The first is the "terrible 2's". The second is adolescence.

"The bad news is that there are two periods when your children are going to be difficult – the "terrible two's" and adolescence; the good news is that neither lasts forever."

(Darryl Cross)

It is true isn't it?

The two-year-old becomes confident on his or her feet, begins to run everywhere, explores everything, gets into everything and has started to use language especially that little word "no". In a sense, he starts to flex his muscles, becoming his own little person strutting his independence. Although it's not verbalised, it's something like "I'll do it my way!" or "I've got rights too!" In turn, the moms and dads or guardians seem to use the same one word relentlessly -- you guessed it, "No!" This is typically followed by other such well used phrases including "Don't do that!"; "Naughty"; "You mustn't...."

Adolescence is the other period where the "muscles" are being flexed and the limits tested. This is the period when the teenager wants to be a man or woman -- to be independent and to "do it my way", "it's my life anyhow!" and "I have my rights!"

"A boy becomes an adult years before his parents think he does, and about two years after he thinks he does."

(General Lewis Hershey; 1911-1977, US Army)

It is probably true to say that this whole notion of independence is the cause for more arguments, fights, and conflict between parents and adolescents than any other area.

On the one hand, there is the adolescent who wants to be his or her own person. On the other hand, there is the parent who is concerned about their child's welfare, safety and protection.

From the adolescent's perspective, the parent is seen as over-bearing, too protective, a worrier and a plain old "kill joy."

From the parent's perspective, the adolescent is seen as wanting to bend the rules, is pushing buttons, being disrespectful, and generally difficult to manage.

The "independence" issue is fought on many battle lines including….
- socialising and going out including aspects such as where the adolescent is going and with whom
- what time the adolescent should be home
- dress style
- homework (or lack of it)
- use of alcohol
- use of the family car
- pocket money or allowance
- how the adolescent keeps their room
- who their friends are
- what they do with their time and what they do with their money

Indeed, it is a fertile ground for many an argument and many a conflict.

John was brought along by his parents because at 14 years of age, he was becoming a handful and "bucking the system." His father had had enough of him and his mother was quite teary and desperate.

Through discussion, it appeared that John was certainly pushing the boundaries and testing limits. He was going AWOL after school, spending time in the city mall with his friends, not arriving home when he said he would and so on.

I asked John's parents to leave the room and calmly announced to John that clearly he was trying to be his own man and a young adult, but that his parents just did not know how to allow him to do so. John smiled and looked relieved.

I wasn't about to tell him off or lecture him just now.

However, I told him that it was his job to be smarter than he was – he clearly wanted to be his own person, but he hadn't demonstrated that to those around him. He certainly gave all the hallmarks of being a young adult, but he had failed to effectively show that to his family and those who mattered.

What could he do to show his parents that he was his own person who could be responsible and independent?

Not surprisingly, he came up with all the kinds of notions and ideas that his parents would have wanted, but were not currently getting.

Yet it is certainly true to say that the adolescent must learn to be independent and in turn, the parent must learn to let go.

Many parents can't wait for the day when their teenagers are independent and have left home and I think I can say with certainty that I have never met a parent who has set a goal for their adolescent to be remaining at home with them indefinitely!

So, the independence has to occur for everyone's sake.

Elena had been seeing me on a random basis for just over ten years. She was now 30 years of age. She was 20 years of age when I first saw her.

She explained that she was born in Australia, but that her parents were from southern Europe. They had fairly strict ideas about how to manage Elena and her sister who was 3 years older. To say that her parents were protective is an understatement. They monitored her constantly. When the parents went out for a Sunday afternoon drive, they would demand that both the daughters go with them.

Elena said that she felt like she was treated as a 5-year-old and that her parents did not trust their daughters. She had never been out with a male although her mother had invited a young man around for dinner one evening and had invited a couple of others over for afternoon tea and coffee. In short, Elena felt caught and trapped. She presented as depressed and had a few medical ailments that reflected her emotional condition.

If she hinted at leaving at all, her mother would fain sickness and ill-health. In fact, when Elena's sister did leave at some point, the mother feigned a heart attack and hospitalisation.

Asked how her parents thought that Elena would eventually leave home and become independent, she said that her parents believed that somehow a man would come along and marry her and then she would leave home, and everything would be just as it should be.

How do parents let go?

Step-by-step in a gradual and planned fashion.

It is inconceivable that once the adolescent turns 18 that he or she should suddenly be independent and self-sufficient. Unfortunately, I have certainly met some parents who have adopted a policy of being really restrictive and protective and then all of a sudden at the magical age of 18 years (it used to be at 21 years of age some decades back) have expected their adolescent to be mature, wise and responsible and act like a thinking adult.

It is probably not hard to guess that the opposite occurs. In other words, once the individual has been bound up in a kind of captivity for a good deal of time and the gates are suddenly opened and they have their new-found freedom, they tend to go berserk and not know how to handle the freedom that they have been given. These adolescents often blow themselves up with alcohol, substance abuse, sexual misconduct and a wild kind of living.

Instead, it is important for parents to gradually release the hold that they have on their adolescents and allow their children to slowly learn to take responsibility and be independent.

In the early teenage years, the independence issue can often surround the adolescent wanting to go out by herself with their peers without parental supervision as would have happened when they were much younger. For example, there may be a request for the teenager to go to the movies with her friends.

As an aside, I am not in favor of teenagers asking if they can "hang around" in the local shopping centre or in the city mall or wherever. This only creates a setting for the teenager to break their boredom by undertaking some antisocial or mischievous behavior. It is not to be encouraged. It is also true that in this case, the parent has little or no idea what the teenager is doing, whom they are with and again, this lack of knowing on behalf of the parent is a major concern.

However, back to our example of *going to the movies*. The following steps need to occur:

> **(1)** There needs to be **a sensible discussion** about where the cinema is, what the movie is, who is going, what time the movie starts and ends and most importantly, how they intend to get there and get home again. All these details need to be very specific and clearly understood by both the adolescent and parents.

> If your adolescent accuses you of being too pedantic or fussy or "over the top," then simply inform them that that's the way it is; you know that you're an old fuss pot and if they want to go to the movies, they'll have to put up with it because you're not going to change!

> **(2)** If the adolescent does not know the answer to each of these questions, then it is important to **teach her that part of being responsible is knowing the answers to these questions**. What do they have to do to find out the answers? Who do they have to talk to? Without the answers, the adolescent needs to understand that the idea of going to the movies is not going to happen.

If she says that she is too embarrassed to find out these answers, then tell her that she has a choice to either face her embarrassment and work through it or not go to the movies.

(3) The arrangements for the movie outing are agreed to and clearly understood. This process however, may need to be negotiated and some compromise may have to be reached, but more will be said about this below.

Sometimes, the arrangements might need to be written down or written onto the family calendar which often is stuck onto the fridge or hangs in the kitchen somewhere. Putting it to paper can be important because we all have "selective listening" at times!

(4) The adolescent is given the opportunity to **go to the movies** and comply with what was originally discussed and agreed to.

(5) If the adolescent behaves responsibly and keeps to her part of the agreement, make sure that you as the parent **praise your teenager** for acting as she said she would and reinforce the notion that she is demonstrating responsibility, earning your trust and starting to show that she can be independent.

(6) If, for whatever reasons, your teenager does not keep to the agreement, **inform her that she has not earned your trust** and that next time there will be no movies or else, there will be limits on where she goes and with whom. Don't make the mistake though, of bawling her out in front of her peers and belittling her in front of her friends.

Maybe you can act quietly and be subdued, but save your "discussion" until later when it is private and maybe when you have had a chance to calm down too.

(7) If your teenager not only did not keep to the agreed arrangements, but also was involved in some irresponsible or poor behavior (e.g. after the movie went for a walk down the shopping mall where one of her friends was picked up for shop-lifting), then there may be some logical consequence that could occur (e.g. the whole group are taken to the police station and questioned) and on your part, there may be **a specific consequence** that is implemented (e.g. grounded for the next three weeks).

Let's take another example when ***your teenager wants to have a party***. Of course, this depends on the age of the teenager and while younger teenagers may comply with the kinds of suggestions below, older teenagers may wish to negotiate on some of these matters.

First and foremost, there needs to be a discussion about the specifics of what will occur. This can't be emphasized enough. Many arguments and conflicts occur between adolescents and their parents because of misunderstanding or because somebody thought somebody else said this or meant to say that or somebody did not hear what the other party had to say and so on.

Through the discussion with your adolescent work out the following:
- How many are to be invited and who they are
- What time the party will start and end

- Indicate clearly to your teenager that the party occurs as long as he is prepared to help prepare beforehand and to clean up afterwards – otherwise it is not on – and be specific about what it is that you need help on
- All visitors naturally will be expected to obey the house rules about smoking and respecting your property for example
- Let him know that any alcohol will be taken away (and that includes soft drink bottles that might have alcohol added)
- As a courtesy, let the neighbors know that there will be a party occurring and let your teenager know prior to the party that the music will be going off at a particular time (e.g. midnight) – work out who will contact the neighbors and which neighbors will be contacted
- Let your adolescent know that the bedrooms are off-limits (in fact, it is a good idea if possible to let younger children play in the bedrooms so that the teenagers do not have access)
- Let your teenager know that you intend to Invite another couple of parents over for help (and moral support and to create a general parental presence)
- When there are a few parents around it is easy to occasionally be able to check the boundaries and the garden area
- Keep an eye on proceedings in a discrete way by taking in the occasional plate of food or goodies
- Do not allow any gatecrashers to enter even if somehow, they thought they had an invitation

With adolescents, planning has to occur – making plans on the run simply does not work and leaving it

all to the last minute is another recipe for disaster. This is no way to show the adolescent how to start to be independent, responsible and organized.

How do you resolve conflict when it occurs?

In this whole process of letting go and showing your teenager how to be independent, it is not surprising that conflicts often arise.

Many parents feel that all the adolescent does is "take, take, take" and that he or she wants it all their own way all the time. Of course, life is a two-way street, but how to get this message over to your teenager can sometimes be a challenge.

Listed below therefore is a **step-by-step approach** to help settle differences of opinion between parents and adolescents.

Let us take the example of a clash with a teenage son who wishes to buy a motorbike against his mother's or father's wishes. Overall, you need to work out and plan your strategy.

(1)   **Try to work out your own attitude and feelings about the situation *before* you approach your son.** Do your own homework first and get it clear in your own mind. Having it clear means that you are less likely to go off on a tangent or "rant and rave" or give a lecture. Completing this sentence below can help you to clarify in your mind what you really feel and think:

a) *I feel*.... (describe your feelings – e.g. "I feel angry, afraid..."etc.)

b) *when you*..... (describe the situation, e.g. "...when you want to buy a motor bike...")
c) *because*..... (describe why you feel that way, e.g. "...because motor bikes give no protection in an accident and I've seen some horrible injuries from motor bike accidents").

(2)   Decide whether the particular situation is worth having all this fuss and bother about. Do I really need to raise the issue? List several reasons why the issue is worth raising, and why it may not. Rate your reasons on the star system (***** meaning very important to * meaning trivial). Do the reasons for tackling the issue outweigh the reasons for not, or it is finely balanced in the middle? The example above might go like this:

Reasons for talking to my son about his desire to buy a motorbike:
He may be injured or killed
        (there is a high risk)   *****
He can't really afford one   **
Motorbikes are associated with bikies and rough types   *

*Reasons for **not*** talking to my son about buying a motorbike:

There will be another awful blow-up between us ****
He'll do as he pleases anyway *
He needs some transport and he certainly can't afford a car   ***

(3)   Decide on the spirit in which you will raise the matter. What kind of manner do I want to present? This protects you from going in with guns drawn or guns blazing and means that you're not going to be defeated before you start.

For example, I want to deal with it.... (firmly, forcefully, mildly, etc.)

(4) **Approach your teenager at an appropriate time** (not when they are rushing out the door to meet their friends or go on a social outing).

a) Begin by telling him how you feel, and why (see step (1) above)

b) Avoid expressing your feeling as criticisms or attacks which will make him defensive and/or aggressive (e.g. "Why can't you be more responsible?" "What's the matter with you?")

(5) **Listen to his reply and check your understanding of:**

a)   his feelings of the situation; and

b)   his reasons for them.

Follow this formula and say: "What you are saying is that you feel....because...." and see if you have his point of view clear in your mind. *Don't rush this step*; it is critical that the adolescent feels heard. This can't be stressed enough.

(6) **Work out a practical agreement or compromise,** if you can. It may be difficult, sometimes impossible; but it is more likely that you'll find a solution if you acknowledge his feelings, explain yours, and discuss matters quietly and calmly, and with goodwill.

If, for whatever reasons, the conversation does get out of hand, don't stay to engage in guerrilla warfare where both of you end up feeling badly and feeling wounded. Retreat. Say that obviously neither of you are communicating well at the moment and you think that you should come back to it later.

If possible, set a time when you can discuss it again, otherwise say that you'd like to clear it up within about 24 hours.

As adolescents think that they are old enough to leave the nest and fly, it is the parent's responsibility to allow them to flap their wings within the safety of the nest.

From there, they undertake small hops from twig to twig and branch to branch before the parent and adolescent is confident enough for them to fly from tree to tree and to be completely independent where "the sky's the limit."

Interestingly, my experience also shows if that process is effective, adolescents do leave home, but many of them return again for extended periods of time!

After all the drama of them struggling to be independent, some come back to the nest anyway for brief periods of time between relationships or jobs or trips overseas!

Life is an interesting paradox is it not – the more you let go, the more they want to come home!

CHAPTER 3 SUMMARY

Independence

Adolescence is where the "muscles" are being flexed and the limits tested. This is the period when the teenager wants to be a man or woman.

How do parents let go?

Step-by-step in a gradual and planned fashion.

How do you resolve conflict when it occurs?

A six-step process is developed as a way of reaching compromise.

CHAPTER 4

Identity: The Task of Adolescence

I remember reading a cartoon about a young man called Randall who was in the middle of his adolescence and was being interviewed about his overall experience. The interview went something like this:

Interviewer: "Now Randall, how long have you been an adolescent?"
Randall: "Um...let's see...I started when I was fourteen...so that makes it two years now."
Interviewer: "I notice that your face is all pimply – is that one of the side effects?"
Randall: "Oh yeah, one of the first. You can try all them creams and stuff, but they don't work...you're just wastin' your money."
Interviewer: "You also seem very self-conscious."
Randall: "Sure...and I'm physically awkward and gangly. It's the hormones – you grow like crazy overnight. And I've got hair in places I didn't know I had before."

Interviewer: "And how has your adolescence affected your relationship with your parents?"
Randall: "Oh, we really don't get on at all, really – I can't relate to them anymore. You know I reckon they're real dumb."
Interviewer: "Well thanks for your time Randall. Before you go, do you have any advice for other youngsters out there who might be on the verge of becoming an adolescent?"
Randall: "Yeah – Don't do it! It's just not worth it, it really isn't…"

Maybe you know someone like Randall. Maybe your own experience was similar to that of this young man.

Having said that, it also needs to be said that for most teenagers, they certainly survive their identity crises in their middle to late teens. Some others though, seem to need to go into their early or middle 20s before they are able to resolve their issues.

The term "adolescence" comes from the Latin word *"adolescens"* which refers to a young man or woman who is growing up in understanding and maturity. This is the real task of adolescence.

"Adolescent development is characterized throughout by oscillating progressions, regressions, and standstills."

(Dr Peter Blos; US Psychoanalyst)

It is a stage

Parents ought to console themselves that this time called **adolescence is not forever!** You can rest assured that it does come to an end. Admittedly, it may not come soon enough for some parents, but it does end.

However, there are some interesting trends in relation to the timing of it all.

First, it seems to be starting earlier now. Research from the United Kingdom where 14,000 young people were surveyed, indicated that puberty was now showing itself at 8 years of age for 1 in 6 young people, whereas at that age 25 years ago, it was only 1 in 100. It is starting earlier. Nice thought isn't it?

Secondly, if it is starting earlier now, where does it end you might ask? Research shows that adolescents are staying home longer (because of tertiary, college and university fees, the high cost of living, and high unemployment rates in some areas) such that they are now leaving home at around 28 years of age.

And you thought that this adolescence thing was just going to be half a dozen years or so!

Traditionally though, it seems to end, allowing for individual differences, at the magical age of 21 years. Then, theoretically, the young person and the parents have both survived. There is even a special party or occasion to celebrate that everyone has survived and largely kept their sanity and the young adult is then given the key to the front door which they have probably had anyway for a decade or so.

Adolescence heralded by physical changes

When a child moves into adolescence, there are **two main changes** that occur.

Firstly, the child develops **biologically**. You know the scenario; hair arrives in strange places and bumps begin to form on the body to fill out the figure and of course, at puberty, children have the ability to reproduce the species (and some unfortunately do!).

"Boys do not grow up gradually. They move forward in spurts like the hands of clocks in railway stations."

(Cyril Connolly; 1903-74, British Journalist)

Secondly, the child develops **mentally**. His or her brain trips over so that they are now able to engage in what is called "hypothetical deductive reasoning" or "abstract reasoning" where they can think and reason like an adult and engage in lateral thinking. Prior to this their thinking was largely concrete, practical, literal thinking.

For example, if a child saw something in a shop that he or she wanted and liked, the child response would be something like, "I want it….and I want it now" (and if I don't get it now, I'll stack on a big turn or a massive temper tantrum).

As an adult, seeing something that you want in a shop, an adult response could be, "I'll need to save up for that," "Maybe I can put it on lay-by" or "I'll get someone to give it to me for my birthday" or "I'll just do without it because there are other things that I need."

Another example is in relation to time. Have you ever noticed that children really have no concept of time?

In other words, their mental capacity does not allow them to understand or comprehend what it means to wait a day, a week or a month. To children, having to wait a week or a month is like having to wait forever. They are not able to differentiate between the two. Time is really parcelled into either "now" or "later."

Ever gone on an extended car journey with a child; no sooner have you gone a few blocks from home and the child asks, "When are we going to get there?" and continues to ask.

As adults, we are able to conceptualise and comprehend what it means to be able to wait a number of hours, or a month, or six months or whatever. We are able to grasp the meaning of what that entails. This is because we are able to think more abstractly and conceptually than our young children who are very literal, concrete and straightforward.

"Adolescence is a period of rapid changes. Between the ages of twelve and seventeen for example, a child may see his parents age twenty years."

(Author Unknown)

These are different ways of thinking and it is not until about 11-13 years that neurologically, the child has the benefit of being able to think more abstractly, problem-solve and reason more like an adult might.

This is why issues like career guidance and thinking about the future are able to be tackled in secondary school or high school whereas beforehand, such issues would be largely inappropriate to tackle.

A murky period

In many other communities and cultures, the physical changes of adolescence are celebrated or ritualized by a kind of passing-out (or passing-in) parade or a kind of graduation.

For instance, in some tribal communities, the child who reaches puberty is given a hunting device or tool by the village elders and told to go out and survive, live off the land, kill a wild beast, and build a hut or shelter in the wilderness. When the child returns, the village says something like, "We will no more call you 'Little Rock,' instead, we will call you 'Mountain Rock' because you have earned your place as an adult in the tribe." This is a puberty rite and it is a clear rite of passage from childhood into adulthood.

The Jewish people have the Bar Mitzvah.

In the Bible, there is a good account of Jesus going through his Bar Mitzvah where he sat in the temple learning his catechism and where he challenged the rabbis.

In our western community, however, this rite of passage has been lost and we have no rituals or celebrations that raise our consciousness about puberty and entering adolescence.

Hence, it's a somewhat murky period that children seem to muddle into and struggle through.

Identity is at the core of this stage called adolescence

With the biological and mental developments which come with puberty, the teenager enters what is called the **"identity crisis."** This is what adolescence is really all about and why it is such an important phase in our development.

As teenagers move into adolescence, they say "goodbye" to their childhood. Part of them wants to say goodbye and part of them wants to hold on to what they have known. **It is an ambivalent period**. Stepping out, but holding on. Looking forward, but looking back.

"Why can't all the problems of adolescence hit us when we're about 24 when we know everything."

(Author unknown)

Their parents are no longer their heroes or protectors and instead, they rely more on what their peers say and do rather than what their parents advise. They dress differently rather than relying on the clothes that their parents lay out or bought for them. They listen to music and radio stations that are different from their parents. They listen to their iPods while at the same time they converse with others where their parents would like their undivided attention. They communicate via text messages and email while their parents use the telephone to talk or catch up personally.

With this move from childhood into adolescence comes a loss, a deep loss.

Gone are the days of certainty when life was seemingly simpler, with fewer major decisions and more security. With the loss comes a kind of struggle. Along with the struggle come the feelings of anger and hard on its heels often come the feelings of depression (but not clinical depression).

In a way, the anger is a mask – a mask for the loss and the confusion that they are going through.

The anger is also about the adolescent now having the mental and biological capacity to be an adult, but not having the control or the means to bring it about. They are still residents in their parents' home and are not the final arbitrators or decision makers.

Because teenagers now have the capacity to engage in adult-type thinking (i.e. abstract and logical reasoning), they start to ask questions about who they are and about their future.

This is why this stage is typically filled with so much anxiety, stress and emotional upheaval. They start to think about their careers, their future life, leaving home and going it alone.

All big issues – all scary issues. All issues about which there are no clear cut answers. All issues that require the individual to take a journey – a journey, in a sense, into the unknown. All issues that require discovery and self-examination. Not easy issues.

There are basically *3 key questions* that adolescents need to ask and find answers for:

"Who am I?"
"Where am I going?"
"Who are all these people around me?"

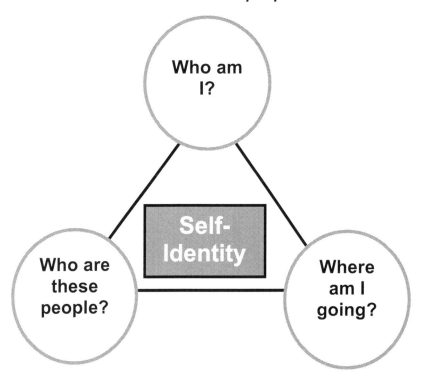

These are critical questions for all of us.

For the adolescent, he or she needs to start to become independent emotionally, and in order for this to happen, he or she needs to consider leaving home in order to successfully answer these key questions.

Hence, it's easy to see why this stage of growing up can be so stormy and rocky.

As I said earlier, irrespective of whether we find our identity or not, life continues on. But, life is much more of a struggle if we do not know who we are and if we have not formed our identity during adolescence. Of course, we move into adulthood, but we are really ill-equipped to handle the struggles and difficulties, as well as the routines of life, if we have not worked out who we are, and how we fit into the scheme of things.

Clinical experience as a psychologist shows me that if the 3 basic questions are **not** successfully answered in adolescence, then life is such that they tend to come back and haunt the individual in later years in the form of what is frequently called a **"mid-life crisis."**

Think about it.

The mid-life crisis occurs and the conservative engineer leaves his job to become a wood turner or the life insurance sales manager throws in his career to become an artist.

If you really get along side these people, you learn that these are their real talents, their burning issues, their inner passions which have been simmering for a long time, and maybe since adolescence.

Identity is built by four primary factors

(1) "Love": boy meets girl – girl meets boy

The first contributing factor in finding an identity has to do with love. Establishing some kind of love relationship with somebody is critical to working out who we are.

Our identity is really only authenticated as we love somebody who also loves us and loves us as unconditionally as it is possible to love.

In other words, having someone love us, warts and all, and love us for who we are, is very powerful – almost mind-blowing.

This is a very potent identity factor because there is an acceptance of us as a person.

Of course, it is debatable whether the adolescent really knows what love is (some adults are not sure either).

Irrespective, whether it is "puppy love" or any other sort of love, the adolescent feels a strong affiliation and attraction towards another of the opposite sex and that feeling is reciprocated. It is a two-way street. And it's just the biggest buzz. So powerful.

"Boys will be boys. And even that wouldn't matter if only we could prevent girls from being girls."

(Anthony Hope; 1863–1933, British Author)

A delightful young woman was feeling depressed and unsure of her way in life. It was almost as if she had lost her way. She was 16-years of age and taking Year 11 at a private co-ed college. In our first session, we touched on the issues that confronted her including her impending final Year 12, her indecision about subject choices, and her lack of career direction beyond secondary school.

Towards the end of our session, she also mentioned that her school's formal was approaching and that she had had her eye for some time on a particular young man in Year 12. We briefly discussed how she might go about asking this particular male to go to the school formal with her.

At the second session, I was prepared to explore more deeply the personal issues that were confronting this young woman.

However, to my surprise, she presented quite differently to what I had seen previously. She was cheerful, smiling, spontaneous and quite outgoing. She reported that after a few false starts in ringing this young man's phone number, she had actually persevered and asked him to the formal. Of course, he had readily agreed. She was over the moon.

Naturally, there was little point in discussing the original issues with which she initially presented. She was in no mood to examine those original issues.

Instead, we talked about boy-girl relationships and the up-coming school formal and I suggested to her that she might like to return when she felt that she wanted to discuss the original issues again. She left my consulting rooms still beaming and smiling. Michael was going to the school formal with her!

Interestingly, her parents thought that I had provided some miracle therapy and were terribly impressed that their daughter had got over her woes. But, I had nothing to do with it -- it was simply the power of love!

The impact of "love" or mutual attraction cannot be underestimated. In a sense, it is the same kind of factor that counselors and therapists call "unconditional positive regard" when it is provided in a clinical counseling setting.

Of course, an adolescent expects that mom and dad love them – that's what they are "paid" to do – that's their job! Incidentally, the other persons outside the family who can provide this unconditional love are the **grandparents**. Don't underestimate the very powerful influence that grandparents can play by the love they give; unconditional love.

> **"Maybe I'm okay after all. Although there are times when I think that I'm not good enough and that I don't measure up, here is my peer telling me that I'm OK, that he really likes me, so I guess that means that I must be OK."**

When someone outside the family though, like a peer (and especially someone from the opposite sex) affirms who he or she is as a person, it is like winning the lottery. It lifts self-esteem. It raises self-confidence. It lifts mood. It makes the person just feel great. Life is so wonderful.

(2) Work: earning a dollar

The second identity factor concerns work. Every researcher who has studied and written about adolescence has reported that the quickest way to improve adolescent self-esteem and to promote self-identity is to get them out to work.

When adolescents work, they usually see an outcome for their day's effort. They see a result; they see what they have accomplished. This certainly makes them feel better than gathering on street corners or in shopping malls or just hanging out.

James had dropped out half way through his final Year 12. He did not like school and felt that Year 12 was either too difficult or too boring or both. He also was having clashes with his teachers and was falling behind in his work. He was not doing any homework or handing up any assignments. He said that he was going to leave and get a job.

At the end of the year, except for doing some odd laboring jobs for his father's friend, he had no work. He was despondent. He said that initially being out of school was great. The odd jobs he had done were OK and he certainly liked receiving a wage from it.

Lately though, he reported that he had just been hanging around at his friends' places and sometimes they went down to the shopping mall, but because he had no cash, he couldn't do much.

He even thought about returning to school!

When you work, you earn a wage. You earn a dollar. Because money is power in our culture, work has a sense of power attached to it as well as providing a sense of achievement.

Money gives the freedom to do what we want, it gives us power and it makes us feel good to get money and to spend money.

For the adolescent, having some hard-earned money in the pocket, not money handed out by mom or dad, gives a sense of pride and sense of being his or her own person.

> **"It's my money and I can spend it how I want. I can buy the music that I want and the clothes that I want."**

Finally, work also allows us to gain a sense of who we are, what our strengths might be and who all these people around us might also be. Work helps us to learn how to relate to others and how to relate to people in our workplace with whom ordinarily we would not perhaps want to associate!

It helps us to relate to many different types of people, e.g. the 'bullies', the 'whiners', the 'blamers', the 'gossips' etc as well as the 'nice' people and in doing so, we understand a little better who we are and our place in the scheme of things.

Have you ever noticed too, that those adolescents who seem to be developing sound self-esteem are often keen to get a casual or part-time job? Those who are floundering or feeling insecure or have a sense of inferiority rarely put their hands up for work of any nature.

If your adolescent wants to work, don't stand in the way, providing of course, that such does not interfere with their studies.

For example, working a shift or two a week (say, for 3 hours one night of the week and on weekends) at a hot bread outlet or fast food chain for example, appears to be about the amount of time with which most adolescents can cope and juggle their studies. In the final Year 12 though, it may be time to give the casual work a rest, since at that stage, it is more important to get those necessary points or scores in order to gain entrance into a tertiary course, traineeship, apprenticeship or training course of some kind.

Having had a year or two of work under their belt however, it sets them up for re-entering the workforce again after secondary school or high school has finished.

Work promotes self-esteem and is important in the identity process.

(3) Friends: who you hang around with

The third identity factor has to do with friends. Having a group of friends to socialize with means that adolescents gain a sense of who they are in relation to those around them.

They gain an awareness of their own self as their identity is verified or matched by the opinions of friends who surround them. In other words, it is very difficult to be able to know who you are in a vacuum remote from others around you. Friends help you to understand yourself.   In a real sense therefore, the choice of friendship group is also very important.

In relation to friends, parents frequently become very concerned about the influence of what is called **the peer group**. It is certainly true, that the tendency to conform to the group, especially the same-sex group, increases during the early part of adolescence, peaking around 13 to 17 years before waning. In the initial stages around early teens, there is a kind of novelty in growing up and reaching the teenage years.   This introduction into adulthood means that some adolescents dive into the process headlong almost abandoning all the so-called common sense that they had before regarding their dress sense, their language and their music for instance.

Generally speaking though, it is important to understand that children grow past that peak of group conformity and start to think for themselves again in later adolescence. This may be a relief for some parents to learn. **It often seems that all the good work that parents thought they were putting into raising their children is suddenly being swept away by the influence of the peer group.** However, it does return. Such common sense does not desert the teenager for ever.

Interestingly, when the peer group is playing a very dominant role in an adolescent's life, there is generally a lack of attention from, and poor relationship with, the parents.

In other words, adolescents who are very peer-oriented are more likely to hold negative views of themselves and/or their friends, and to report less affection, support and discipline at home. In contrast, an adolescent with good self-confidence is in a better position to choose his or her own values, independently of the peer group which, in the long run, is the essence of finding one's own identity.

Meg was a 15-year-old who was staying out at night and sleeping over at her boyfriend's house. She was known to have been climbing out of her bedroom window in the early hours of the morning when she was 13 and 14 years old and meeting friends to "hang out."

Her school attendance was sporadic and she often skipped school if her friends decided that they would go down to the local shopping mall for the day or ride the trains all day or even go into the city. Her mother reported that Meg had always been a problem in that as a single mum, she had to leave Meg with either her sister (when she was available) or her own mother.

Meg's mother said that she too had to lead her own life as well as work. Life overall had "been a bit hectic" in that she had had a number of relationships and had recently "kicked out" her de facto who had become violent. At this stage though, she did not know what to do with Meg and thought that she would now consult an "expert."

If the peer group influence seems to be a major problem, the real issue may lie much closer to home, and that's where the solution will need to be found too.

Furthermore, parents need to understand that on many issues, the peer group's values will be largely similar to theirs as parents because adolescents tend to pick friends from similar family backgrounds to their own. The peer group's influence however is most likely to be in the area of dress, music, entertainment, expectations over going out, and use of language. If you think about it, these are not critical life and death decisions. Sure, at times they seem paramount and it may really irritate you as a parent, but the reality is that they are not necessarily so important.

(4) Being good at something: anything

We all know that being good at something certainly helps you feel good. When others also acknowledge and recognize that you are good at something, it really gives a boost to your ego.

It doesn't matter what it happens to be. An adolescent could show a particular talent in fixing and racing remote controlled cars or planes; she could be exceptionally good on the BMX bike track. The adolescent might really enjoy being in the school choir or the school play; he could be a whiz on the computer with either designing web-sites or taking the computer apart and altering the hardware; or be really good making things with her hands such as using a welder or cooking. Often, the adolescent shows real talent in sports whether it be football, netball, tennis, swimming, soccer, squash, judo or athletics.

There is little doubt that having a talent and having it recognized does wonders for self-esteem and adds to the individual's identity.

As a parent, it is important to look for any sign where the adolescent might show some talent. In some instances, it is a case of taste and see. It is not always clear where an adolescent's strengths might lie so it may require some experimentation.

In early adolescence for example, it might be a case of trying out for the tennis team, of seeing whether art as a subject appeals, perhaps joining the scouts, girl guides or lifesaving clubs, or enrolling for a computer course. Some adolescents that I have seen have been avid readers and know particular authors off by heart and are happy to chat about the books they have read. I have seen adolescents who have been very skilled at chess. It has generally been a parent with whom they first played and learnt the rules, but graduated into chess clubs once they started to beat mom or dad! The adolescent might be really good with people and have a "knack" with others; in this case, they might consider school leadership positions or else get a part-time or casual job where their people skills could flourish and be developed even further.

Remember, this is not a time for the parent to re-live their own adolescence and push their own preferences or biases. You as a parent have had your turn. Now stand back and watch. Talk to your teenager about having some fun in various areas. What would he like to try? What do you see might be her strength? Let him or her know that they are not locked in – this is the time of experimentation, for trying out.

Every adolescent I have ever known has always had a particular strength or talent. Some are more obvious than others, but talents are *always* present.

The playing out of various roles

Because adolescence is about finding an identity (Who am I?), it is not unusual for an adolescent to try various roles. They experiment for instance, in trying to be different from their parents and they may try out different religions too. In a sense, they have only known the roles of those closest to them, e.g. their father, mother or carers, and while they may love and respect mom and dad, they may also want to test out how far they can go. They experiment therefore with other roles and ideas.

For example, a teen may get her hair cut or styled in various ways. One of my clients, a 15-year-old spent $300 and 7 hours having her long hair tightly braided by two African hairdressers. They may also engage in body piercing such as a nose stud or multiple rings through their ears. These actions are designed essentially to show that they are now different from their parents. Sometimes these kinds of actions shock the parent, but the essential message is, "Look at me now, I'm my own person, I'm growing up, I'm an adult already."

We are all merely players strutting our stuff at a particular time and place. We often play many parts or roles.

It was Shakespeare who said,

"All the world's a stage,
And all the men and women merely players:
They have their exits and their entrances;
And one man in his time plays many parts...."

Probably it's true to say though, that the biggest danger in playing out various roles during this period is that the individual teenager doesn't come to any consensus about who he or she actually might be and instead, simply goes through life playing a whole bunch of different roles.

One day he puts on one hat and another day, he puts on another hat – and they end up being phony, perhaps a "con man," perhaps being shallow or superficial, but certainly not real.

Do you know any adults like this?

For the adolescent, and for all of us, finding out who we are means playing various roles, but through that process, we come to an abiding sense of inner saneness and sameness that is also matched by the opinions, thoughts and feelings of the other significant people who surround us in life.

It's not a smooth transition

Anna Freud (Sigmund Freud's daughter) said, "It is normal for an adolescent to act in an un-permissible manner; to love his or her parents on the one hand, while on the other hand, to hide from them when they bring his or her lunch or gym clothes or whatever to school." Freud said that at any other time of life such behavior would be considered "crazy," but in adolescence, it's considered "normal."

In other words, this period is one of up and down, this way and that. There are no clear formulas, no clear guidelines, no clear pathways. The adolescent can be so grown up one day and so childlike the next.

One day he'll want to give the parent a big hug and the next he'll walk out without even saying goodbye. One day she wants the parent to go shopping with her, the next day she doesn't want to be seen with the parent at all. One day it seems like he has won the lottery and the next it seems like he has just lost a financial fortune. One day she'll help with cleaning her room, the next day it looks like a bomb has hit it. At one period, teenage siblings will get on so well together, but before you know it, they fight like "cat and dog."

In a nutshell, the transition is not smooth because the identity is being worked out. It is not a clear-cut process, formula or recipe.

Just imagine that on your adolescent's door is a sign that says, "Work in Progress." The final product is still being developed.

As parents, we do not judge the result until the work is done and the product refined. Yet we need to continue to love him or her along the way and to maintain our relationship with them.

"Many children grow through adolescence with no ripples whatever and land smoothly and predictably in the adult world with both feet on the ground. Some who have stumbled and bumbled through childhood suddenly burst into bloom. Most shake, steady themselves, zigzag, fight, retreat, pick up, take new bearings, and finally find their own true balance."

(Jane Whitbread; US Writer)

FOOD for THOUGHT

Not only is this stage difficult for adolescents, but around about this time, the parents may also be having their own struggles particularly if they are going through what is commonly called a "mid-life crisis" – the whole family starts to come apart at the seams!

It's a wonder at times that we all survive!

CHAPTER 4 SUMMARY

It is a stage

Parents ought to console themselves that this time called adolescence is not forever.

Adolescence heralded in by physical changes

When a child moves into adolescence, there are **two physical changes** that occur.

Firstly, the child changes **biologically**.

Secondly, the child changes **mentally**. Their brain trips over so that they are now able to engage in what is called "hypothetical deductive reasoning" or "abstract reasoning" where they can think and reason like an adult and engage in lateral thinking. Prior to this their thinking was largely concrete, practical, literal thinking.

A murky period

In our western community, the rite of passage into adolescence has been lost and we have no rituals or celebrations that raise our consciousness about puberty and entering adolescence.

Hence, it's a somewhat murky period that we seem to muddle into and struggle through.

Identity is at the core of this stage called adolescence

In short, there are basically **3 key questions** that adolescents need to ask and find answers for: *"Who am I?"* – *"Where am I going?"* – *"Who are all these people around me?"*

Identity is built by four primary factors

(1) "Love": boy meets girl – girl meets boy
(2) Work: earning a dollar
(3) Friends: who you hang around with
(4) Being good at something: anything

The playing out of various roles

Because adolescence is about finding an identity (Who am I?), it is not unusual for an adolescent to try on various roles. They experiment, for instance, in trying to be different from their parents.

It's not a smooth transition

This adolescent period is up and down, this way and that. There are no clear formulas, no clear guidelines, no clear pathways.

The adolescent can be so grown up one day and so childlike the next. Just imagine that on your adolescent's door is a sign that says, "Work in Progress."

The final product is still being developed.

CHAPTER 5

Talk the Walk & Walk the Talk:
The Task of the Parent

W hat is it that we're really supposed to be doing as parents?

This parenting thing is really difficult to do especially when we are supposed to think on our feet and handle an adolescent who's just as good at thinking on his or her feet if not better than we are.

Adolescents tend to:

• *reject our advice as parents ("dad, you wouldn't know;" "mum, you're out of touch"),*
• *they tell us they know better ("forget it mum, I'm gonna do it this way;" "I'm gonna wear these pants not those dumb pants you reckon"),*
• *they won't do as they are told ("yeah, yeah, I'll do my room later" -- which interpreted means, get off my back right now and hopefully, you'll also forget about it later),*

> • *they'd like to use the home as a hotel / motel, come and go as they please, and expect that the parents will be their slave and clean up after them,*
> • *they want the parents to be on 24 hour chauffeur duty and to respond immediately to their requests to be driven anywhere at any time of the day or night,*
> • *they expect the parents to be a bank where the teenager can make monetary withdrawals at any time they please.*

So, what are the guidelines for being a parent to an adolescent?

1. Keep the relationship going at all times

Keeping the communication open is, at times, very difficult. On occasions, it is almost impossible. On the one hand, you know in your head that you should keep calm and handle the matter in an adult manner, being reasonable and logical. On the other hand, you would gladly like to "do your block," rant and rave, give a lecture and then strangle your adolescent!

When you talk to your adolescent, try not to use "you." It tends to be a blame word, an accusatory word. "You" tends to get people offside straight away and defensive. Hence, questions like "Where have you been?" (because they are late getting home) or "What are you doing?" (because they are not ready in time to go out) are hardly going to lead to an open and honest reply from an adolescent (or many other people). Instead, statements like "I thought we agreed on a time for you to be home?" and "We are due to leave in 5 minutes" are comments that are not as accusatory or blaming.

Sometimes the teenager may not want to talk to the parent at all. They are silent for days on end. The parent gets the cold shoulder.

Of course, it is important that as parents you hear from your teenager, but don't make the mistake of asking too many intrusive questions (e.g. "What's the matter with you, you've been in your room for two days now, what's got into you?"). Instead, make statements such as "I'm frustrated that we're not talking together." Alternatively, you could ask what are called multiple choice type questions such as, "Are you feeling sad or maybe just out of sorts right now?" Don't expect that the adolescent will immediately respond to you, but at least it doesn't sever the relationship or your communication.

2. Be a model

"Do as I say, not as I do" is *not* what it is all about.

As the child gets older and moves into adolescence, parents need to use less power and more *influence*. Being a role model is a powerful, potent teacher. What you do is more important than what you say.

Do you as a parent really understand how powerful the modeling agent is? In my clinical psychology practice, I have often had parents tell me that they decided very early on in the piece that when they had children, they would never treat their own kids in the same way that they had been treated.

For example, they wouldn't yell and scream at their children like their father or mother screamed at them. They would never use phrases like, "Because I'm your father, that's why." Then later, they report that they just can't believe it because they "hear" themselves acting and behaving just like their parents did. Consequently, they feel guilty and feel that they are failing as parents.

The model of the parent is potent. Whether we like to or not, we carry the model of our parents around in our heads even when we are adults ourselves and sometimes even after our own parents have been dead for many years.

Certainly, one thing is clear – if you are inconsistent and you do one thing and say another, guess who is going to recognize that and probably throw it up in your face? What do you think that will do to your credibility as a parent?

If you want your teenager to respect you, then practice what you preach. If you don't want them to abuse alcohol, don't abuse it yourself. If you are concerned about them smoking, then give up yourself. If you are concerned about their use of language and swearing, mind your own tongue. If you don't want them to veg out in front of the television and be a "couch potato", then don't live your life in front of the "box." If you are concerned about them popping pills, then don't be a hypochondriac yourself. If you want them to drive in a safe and reasonable manner, then do so yourself.

"Children have never been very good at listening to their elders, but they have never failed to imitate them."

(James Baldwin; 1861-1934, American Philosopher & Psychologist)

3. Put up sign-posts

It is absolutely vital to make sure that the pathway to be taken by the adolescent is clearly sign-posted.

The signposts give a person a clear indication of whether they are on the right track and what might lie ahead. In fact, it is frequently reassuring to be able to see the signposts and to know that you are still on target and headed towards your destination. Without the signs, the road ahead would be fraught with anxiety, mistakes, frustrations and a waste of time and energy.

So it is in life. In the same way that the road signs show us the way where we are going or plan to go, the guide posts, signs and beacons that parents put up for their teenagers act in the same way. They show children the path ahead and give them guidelines how to get to responsible adulthood.

Guidelines, signs or beacons?

It is certainly the case though, that **there are different kinds of signs.**

For example, as you travel from one destination to another, especially in the country, you will see signs that are often placed on corners or curves in the road which indicate with an arrow what the curve ahead looks like and along with that is usually a number indicating the speed at which the curve can be taken with safety.

In other words, this is a kind of *guideline* which helps you alter your speed and prepare for the corner, although it is certainly true that there is nothing that says that you have to abide strictly by the speed suggested.

For instance, if there is a smooth curve in the road as indicated by the sign and the suggested speed is 45mph, you could take the corner at 40mph or maybe 50mph and still do so safely. The point is that such a sign is a guideline, but one that does not need to be adhered to strictly nor one that does not need to be enforced strictly. Even so, you would be foolish to ignore it altogether.

For our adolescent, these guidelines are about how to be organized, how to arrange a study program, how to be busy and keep active and how to run their lives.

On the other hand, there are *signs* that need to be followed because not to do so could mean danger to life and/or limb.

For example, take the simple "Stop" sign that we see every day in our travels. To ignore this sign could have tragic consequences. I know that we might be in a hurry or find that having to stop is a real nuisance, but the sign is there to protect us and others to make sure that we negotiate the intersection as safely as possible.

For our adolescents, the signs have to do with issues of where they go and with whom, they have to do with alcohol abuse, with driving a car (including who is driving and what to do if the driver is drunk or careless), have to do with strangers and what is appropriate behavior.

Finally, there are *beacons* which we typically see off our coasts.

These are erected to warn of dangers such as reefs, shallow water, rocky protrusions and small islands. They spell danger and in no way can we manipulate them, change them, alter them or somehow get around them. These beacons or light houses are immovable.

For our teenagers, the beacons of life would surround issues of smoking tobacco, drug taking such as marijuana, permissive sex and criminal activity such as shoplifting.

Type of Sign	Example	Life Issue
Guidelines	Curve 45mph	• Study habits • Time management • Organizing themselves • Making it onto the sports team • Helping others in life
Signs		• Where they are going and with whom • Alcohol use • Stranger danger • Protective behaviors
Beacons	Lighthouse 	• Smoking • Drug taking • Permissive sex • Criminal activity

It is important to recognize that guidelines, signs and beacons should always be erected irrespective of whether the teenager follows them or not. The adolescent needs to know the path ahead and how to negotiate it.

Of course, adolescents may rebel and argue about it. But as one adolescent said in a counseling session, "I know I'm stuffing up, but I still want to know what my parents reckon is the right thing to do."

The role of parents is to provide the necessary guidance.

4. Develop their "self-esteem"

This is the most important gift that parents can give to their children. Healthy self-esteem is a kind of "insurance policy" against whatever life has to throw at you. It is at the core of your survival. It is a buffer against life; it is a tool for success.

In my experience, building self-esteem involves two main factors as the diagram below shows:

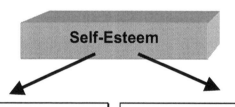

External Factors	Internal Factors
(i.e. that which can be observed or seen; it is easily recognizable)	(i.e. that which is inside the individual and cannot necessarily be seen)
1A. Being good at something	2A. Having positive self-talk
1B. Having good social skills	2B. Having a positive self-picture

Let me take each of these main factors in turn.

1A. Being good at something

Every adolescent I have ever known has been good at something. As a parent or caregiver, it is your responsibility to find out what your adolescent excels at and encourage that particular talent. I have counseled adolescents who have been very talented at, fixing and racing model cars, boats and planes, skate boarding, graffiti, surfing, all kinds of sports, fixing computers, art or design, rap dancing, ballroom dancing and war games. Everything you can imagine I've seen adolescents excel in. Find out what it is and really encourage it. To be good at something and to be recognized for it does wonders for self-esteem.

1B. Having good social skills

Being able to communicate well, especially at the first meeting is a critical skill. Give out good vibes and usually you get back good vibes. This makes you feel good and boosts your self-esteem.

> **"You don't get a second chance to make a good first impression."**

I am constantly surprised how frequently adolescents have not learnt the basic art of smiling, maintaining eye contact, looking a person squarely in the face, saying hello in an audible voice and giving a firm handshake.

Adolescents who know how greet and meet have a flying head start. People generally warm to them instantly. It makes the adolescent feel good and builds self-esteem.

If after the first meet and greet, the adolescent also knows how to hold a conversation, then the self-esteem builds even faster.

Holding a conversation by the way, is **not** being knowledgeable about a whole lot of things such as politics, local events or world affairs. Many adolescents (and many adults!) wrongly believe that in order to be a good conversationalist, you need to know a whole lot of "stuff" or you need to have things in "common." Wrong. Totally wrong.

The secret to holding a conversation is being interested in the other person. **They do the talking. You just listen and ask questions**. Now, that's not meant to sound too simple, but essentially that's the way it is.

I have instructed many adolescents and adults in the art of listening and in asking appropriate questions and they have been amazed at the results. (I have also authored a manual on listening skills written basically for business, but the principles hold no matter what the environment; see the Store at **www.drdarryl.com** and look for "*Listen Up Now*".)

Try it out for yourself and teach your adolescent how to do it; it's about listening and asking questions. It is easy once you know how. What have you got to lose?

2A. Having positive self-talk

We've all heard the question, "Is the glass half empty or is it half full?" It all has to do with a positive attitude.

There is no doubt that being able to think positively is critical to self-esteem. Beating up on yourself, e.g. "I'm no good," "I'm hopeless," "I'll never make it," "I wish I was smart," "I'm so dumb," "I'm a failure" makes you feel badly and act or behave poorly.

"Success doesn't come from the way you think it does, it comes from the way you think."

(Dr Robert Schuller; US Pastor & Author)

Dr Martin Seligman from the University of Pennsylvania has been researching "optimism" and depression for over 20 years and has concluded that positive self-talk was at the core of our self-esteem. His books "Learned Optimism" and "The Optimistic Child" are best sellers.

Unfortunately, our self-talk, sometimes called our internal dialogue or our self-chatter, is something we do so naturally and automatically, it is difficult for us generally to catch ourselves talking negatively to ourselves. However, we do get a glimpse of our self-talk when we talk out loud or when we say things to other people.

Psychologists who practice cognitive behavioral therapy specialize in teaching people including adolescents, how to think positively.

Self-help books like those of Martin Seligman are also readily available. As I've indicated before, I have also written a manual on this whole subject called "*How to*

Stop Your Self-Sabotage: Steps to Increase Your Self-Confidence" which is available at **www.drdarryl.com** .

Changing self-talk lifts self-esteem.

2B. Having a positive self-picture

Believe it or not, the powerhouse under-pinning our self-esteem is how we *see* ourselves.

After many decades in psychology, I now recognize that we all live in our pictures. In other words, we are constantly seeing, imagining and creating pictures in our head that we use our language to describe.

"It is the self-image that governs what a person 'can' and 'can't' do."

(Darryl Cross)

Again, we do this so automatically that we fail to see how critical this is to our existence, our survival and more particularly, to our self-esteem.

These pictures of how we see ourselves are so vital because they act as a kind of automatic pilot for us. They unconsciously guide and direct our actions and behavior.

It is important for us to practice seeing ourselves in a positive light.

These mental training exercises have been used and endorsed by countless famous Olympic and pro-athletes, elite sports men and women, authors, artists, entertainment personalities, business leaders, and others.

They are used today by countless people in all walks of life.

CHAPTER 5 SUMMARY

What is it that we're really supposed to be doing as parents?

1. Keep the relationship going at all times

Keep the communication open at all times; this is very difficult, but important to do.

2. Be a model

"Do as I say, not as I do" is *not* what it is all about.

3. Put up sign-posts

It is absolutely vital to make sure that the pathway or road to be taken by the adolescent is clearly sign-posted.

It is certainly the case though, that **there are different kinds of signs.** There are what we could call **guidelines**, **signs**, and **beacons** and we need to make sure that our adolescent is aware of all three.

4. Develop their self-esteem

Self-esteem is our under-pinning to a successful life. As parents, it ought to be our prime responsibility to do all we can to ensure that we "fire-proof" or "life-proof" our children with a healthy self-esteem.

CHAPTER 6

30 Hints for Dealing with Adolescents

Hints are like handy guidelines. They are not rules. They are not laws. They are hints. Therefore, it is important that parents, foster-parents or guardians work out for themselves, what their adolescent might need. Remember, not all adolescents are the same.

The following 'hints' are not presented in any particular order. In a sense, they are a smorgasbord of options and as such, you can feel free to sample and taste wherever you like.

Of course, there may be nothing to your liking or nothing that takes your fancy. However, there may be one or two morsels which you may like to try which may help your family function better and which may help you in your parenting.

Some of these hints might seem a little harsh or may offend. They are not intended to do so. They may cause some to hesitate.

Try to understand the message that is being portrayed. You are at liberty to sample what you will and you do not have to take on board anything with which you do not feel comfortable.

1. Stay linked to your adolescent.

On this journey through adolescence make it your business to be linked, to **stay "connected."** Preserve your relationship at all costs. Do not get separated. Do not be cut adrift.

A really effective way to stay connected is to do something that you and your adolescent have not done before and where you haven't organized it to the hilt. Have an adventure together.

For example, you might go for an excursion into the alps or a national park or the outback – any place where you are not in control and you are dependent on one another and have to lean on one another and talk to one another.

Try camping, going away for a weekend or bushwalking.

Try a new hobby (e.g. go-Kart racing, remote-controlled model boats, fishing).

Try a new sport (e.g. horse riding, snow or water skiing) or something neither of you have tried before (e.g. a ride in a helicopter, kayaking, riding in a hot air balloon).

I know of one father for example who has three sons and every birthday, he takes a son as a birthday treat on a special "outback" camp and excursion where it is just father and son together.

It has become a family ritual and each of the boys treasure this birthday weekend each year.

It is a special time for them and they feel very proud that it is just them and dad going away for the weekend together.

2. Learn to listen, really listen.

Listening is an almost forgotten skill. We all too frequently say things to our adolescent like, "You're not listening to me" when we haven't heard what our adolescent has said to us in the first place!

The one thing that adolescents complain to me most about their parents is that they don't listen. In fact, **around 7 out of 10 adolescents say that their parents don't listen**.

The mother was quite tearful. She had felt that her son had alienated her for at least six months now and that the situation had grown worse. Whenever she tried to tell him what to do, he would walk out on her.

The son however, said that his mother never listened to him; she was only concerned about getting her own point across and besides, he said that he'd heard it all "a thousand times before."

I suggested that the mother try an experiment. Whenever the son talked about anything, she either had to paraphrase what he had said (e.g. "So what happened was....," "So you felt....," "What you're saying is....") OR the mother had to ask a clarifying question (e.g. "Are you saying that....?", "I'm not sure I caught all that....," "Can you say that again because I'm not sure I understand it?"). The mother had to do this for 14 days.

She returned to say that the situation had eased somewhat. I advised her to continue this routine for another 14 days. Once she had clearly heard her son and he knew he had been heard, then she had earned the right to say her piece in a calm, collected manner.

She came back later to tell me that the tension between them had reduced significantly now and she certainly felt that there was hope for their relationship going forward.

Research has shown that the average teenager has an attention span of about 13.6 seconds! Whatever you have to say therefore, needs to be in short bursts – quick, to the point and said softly.

However, before you point the finger squarely at adolescents, I have read that adults, on average, let the other person talk for about 17 seconds before interrupting!

The message in relation to teenagers is this: don't expect your kids to understand you until you have understood and listened to them.

Someone wise once said, "The Good Lord gave us two ears and one mouth, and we should use them in that proportion."

3. Keep adolescents on the move.

Teenagers are only a problem when they grind to a halt or stop. "Stopping" in this sense doesn't just mean sitting in their darkened room for hours listening to heavy metal music. It also might mean sitting in front of the television for hours at a time or perhaps sitting in front of the computer for hours on end. It also means hanging around on street corners or in shopping malls and arcades doing little that is constructive.

"Adolescent boys often complain that there is nothing to do and then stay out all night doing it."

(Author Unknown)

Both sport and work save lives and save self-esteem. Keep adolescents moving.

This is a time of growth and development when they need to be experimenting, exploring and finding out about themselves. Typically, the best ways to increase self-confidence includes playing sport, working part-time for a wage or having a hobby in which the adolescent excels or shows talent.

I fully remember talking to a 16 year old young man who was an avid collector of motorcar magazines and who knew all the jargon about motorcars, engines and specifications. At 12-years of age, he saw a little old Mini Minor parked on the side of the road with a 'For Sale' sign of $850 on the windscreen.

His parents helped him buy the car, even though he could not legally drive, and over the next four years, he worked on the car religiously. There was a definite sense in which he not only spent his time usefully in this regard, but became an expert on cars in general and this model in particular. There was no doubt that he felt a sense of pride in his accomplishment.

4. Make the rules crystal clear.

Communicate about what the rules are. Negotiate them. Write them out and have the adolescent sign them. Put them onto the pin-board or refrigerator and follow them yourself.

There are more arguments about the *interpretation* of the rules or what one person in the household thought the other said or meant to say than any other area that I know. Frequently, these little misunderstandings blow out into major arguments and conflict. It is simply not worth it – set up the rules beforehand and make them clear.

You need to make sure that the rules are negotiated and agreed upon (see **Appendix 1** for an example of a *contract* that was negotiated with an adolescent). It is critical to get the adolescent's commitment to the rules.

Further, adolescents, as do some parents, have selective listening. It is imperative that the negotiated rules be committed to paper and signed. Otherwise, you'll have an argument over the interpretation of the rules and who wants World War 3 or a Federal Court of Law being conducted in your own house.

"You can tell a child is growing up when he stops asking where he came from and starts refusing to tell where he is going."

(Author Unknown)

A mother complained that her adolescent son would make a terrific lawyer because he argued about everything and she found the ongoing verbal battles tiring. She said that her son was very manipulative and seemed to have an answer for everything.

We worked out a strategy whereby she and her husband would agree on the standards that they wanted in their house and that they would both sit down and talk to their son. They would make the rules black and white rather than grey which had previously set the scene for arguments and battles.

She returned to say that after some initial protest, the negative energy and tension in the household had subsided and things were now running much more smoothly.

She was surprised at the impact that making the rules clear had on the family as well as on herself. She couldn't believe why she hadn't thought of it herself – after all, that was the way she ran her business!

5. Be un-shockable.

Don't let your teenagers knock the living daylights out of you or shock you. Be poker faced. Even though you might be doing cartwheels on the inside from what you might be hearing or it might be turning you grey instantly, **give the impression on the outside that you are unflappable and that you are simply taking it all in your stride**.

Sometimes what adolescents say or do is simply a test anyway.

Nevertheless, let them know that you want to hear **all** of it. Don't be tempted to cut them off in mid-conversation or be tempted to jump in with some "good" advice or a reprimand. Remember you were a kid once and doubtless you got up to some tricks too. Be honest with yourself about your own adolescence (were you really a "goody two-shoes" who never stepped out of line?).

Remember, adolescents need direction with guidelines, signs or beacons.

6. Don't "up" any punishment as a way of trying to get on top of your adolescent.

If you keep erupting like Mount Vesuvius and dishing out the punishments, you will ultimately lose the plot. Your adolescent will also resent you. Your efforts will only throw him or her, and possibly you as well, out of control.

You will also be in a position of having given out such harsh punishments that it will be doubtful that you will be able to enforce the punishment and may have to back down anyway. If you threaten a particular punishment and you don't follow through, then you only sabotage yourself. The adolescent will make a mental note that you don't really mean what you say (that you're 'easy street' or a 'push-over') and act accordingly.

> I recall the father who grounded his son for 6 months because the son was involved with some other youths in shoplifting.
>
> Sure the father was angry and had good reason to be and definitely, the criminal activity that the son was engaged in was highly inappropriate and wrong.
>
> The 6 months grounding through two sets of school holidays, nearly broke the boy's spirit.

Instead, take the opposite tack. Just learn to bite your tongue and sit on your anger. Make the teenager wait for your reaction because having to wait confuses them.

Act **calmly** and listen to their feelings and thoughts about what they are doing and check that they have heard your thoughts.

It is also human nature that if your adolescent has made a mistake, then they would naturally expect you to explode, to dish out a lecture and give a punishment. When you don't automatically follow this procedure, it disarms them.

7. Don't assume physical growth = emotional growth.

Adolescence is a time of rapid physical changes. The hormones kick in and growth occurs in all sorts of ways.

For males, their body fills out and for females, bumps and curves appear and hair grows in all sorts of places for both sexes.

As parents, we sometimes believe that because our adolescent is obviously growing in front of our very eyes, he or she must also be developing emotionally and maturing. Wrong.

I know of one 15-year-old adolescent male who seems very much the macho, "a man's man," who prides himself on being a star footballer for his school, but his mother confided that on some weekends for instance, he still loves to hop into bed with her for a cuddle as he did when he was little.

It may be true that our adolescent is slowly maturing, but don't expect for a moment that emotional development is keeping pace with physical development. Don't be fooled into thinking that because your adolescent is growing up on the outside that they are also growing up on the inside at the same pace.

But some adolescents never grow up emotionally and not surprisingly, we end up with adults who are still just "little boys" or "little girls."

8. Be up-front about puberty.

Don't become anxious where as a parent, you are afraid to discuss sexual matters. Don't let your own hang-ups be passed onto your own children. Many of us were reared in times when sex was hush-hush. It was the outlawed topic. It was something that you just didn't talk about. When we did talk about it, it was with some embarrassment.

Often, if we as children got the message that somehow sex was a definite "no-no," then, all of a sudden, it became attractive to us. It was the "forbidden fruit" and became attractive.

If adolescents take their sexuality underground because it embarrasses you, they may not ever feel comfortable confronting their own sexuality and certainly would find it difficult to confront it with others.

Josie slouched in the arm chair. She wore jeans, tea shirt and a loose fitting coat. She rested her head in her hand as she leaned on one arm of the chair. She looked despondent and down. At 15 years, she had virtually left school and was just "hanging out." She talked about how she often went out and had "one night stands" because she wanted to be loved and held and sex was one way she could get it.

We got onto the topic of sex. Of course, there were many issues in Josie's life, but in relation to sex in particular, she looked at me with a kind of hurt look in her face and said "My mum never talked to me about sex...I think that she was too frightened to...she just left around the odd girlie magazine left open to a story about sex....but she never talked to me about it.....I wish she had....I really wanted her to talk to me."

In a sense therefore, be upfront about it and talk about it. Now that doesn't mean that you have to have "deep and meaningfuls," but from an early age there ought to be an openness about sex. It's easier if you started earlier in life than if you suddenly bring it up later.

9. Guarantee complete confidentiality.

If your teenager does want to talk to you, he or she does not expect you to share their story with Auntie May or the next door neighbor or your circle of friends or whoever.

Adolescents are very concerned about how they are being seen by others (as we all are) and it is very important to them that they look good in the eyes of others. They certainly don't need you passing on their stories that may, in some way, undermine them or make them look poorly.   More importantly, your adolescent needs to trust you and depend on you. You need to keep your word.

I have had more than one adolescent in my office who has told me that they could not trust one or other of their parents to keep a confidence. In those cases, the adolescent typically is saddened that they cannot confide in the parent(s).

It is a deep hurt.

This issue of confidentiality is especially important if the adolescent specifically asks you "not to tell anyone." At this point, you as an adult, have to be on your best behavior.

However, there is one proviso. At some point, your teenager needs to know that you will keep a confidence "except if it is dangerous and then I'll need to talk to someone else about it."

In other words, in rare circumstances, what your teenager may tell you could be to do with criminal activity or to do with endangering someone's life or similar. In this regard, your adolescent needs to know that there are boundaries and that you will not "dob" or "run to the school principal" or "call the cops," but that you will need to consider the options and most probably seek advice from someone else.

This does not necessarily mean that you are going to break the confidence, but you will need to seek advice.

10. Don't expect perfect compliance.

Any teenager who is entirely compliant and who does everything that is asked of him or her is either sick or wants something! It isn't normal!

It is expected that, at times, an adolescent will challenge the parent's authority. This is part of the growing up process where the adolescent 'tests the waters' as the saying goes and tests the limits and boundaries. This is part of "breaking away" and learning what life is all about and working out how she is handling it all.

These challenges to our authority or what we say are often annoying and tiring, but this is how the adolescent is learning to be responsible. It is important that we allow situations to occur that will permit responsible behavior to occur. Do we let them go to that party? Do we agree to them meeting their friends in town? Do we agree to staying out later than was initially discussed?

Of course, there is often a risk factor, but we as parents do all in our power to ensure that the outcome is successful and not the other way round.

11. Forget the "When I was your age..."

Who cares what you did when you were younger. The world couldn't care less! That was then and this is now.

A sure way to turn off your teenager is to start the story with, "When I was your age." If you are concerned about staying in touch with your adolescent and want to maintain communication, drop that notion altogether.

If you really do want to make a point though about your past, a better way to introduce the subject is with, "I recognize myself in you...." or perhaps make it a question like, "Do you know what used to happen with grandpa?" Personalize it. This is certainly much less confronting and doesn't sound like you're about to launch into a lecture (which you probably were).

12. If teenagers flatly refuse to cooperate, refuse to provide goods and services for them.

You should not be expected to provide a 5-star hotel where they can come and go and do as they like. Adolescents have responsibilities and should do chores just like anyone else. Don't fight with them, just starve them out!

This may sound harsh, but every organization and home needs to have its rules and guidelines. Life is not a "free lunch" or a "free ride" and instead, there are obligations and responsibilities. Everyone, including the adolescent, has to learn this.

Where is it written that you have to go on providing services like a slave while your teenager treats you and/or others like dirt? That is simply not acceptable.

Maybe you need to inform your adolescent that, from this point onward, he needs to wash and iron his own clothes, he needs to prepare his own meals, that he no longer has a "right" to the family car or to use the phone whenever he wishes.

After all, you can tell him that you clearly see that he wants to be independent and wants to be his own person. Tell him that you, as the parent, are going to allow him this opportunity – from this point onward, he will take care of himself including food, washing, ironing, cleaning etc.

Of course, once he decides to participate in the family again, then maybe you will be glad to resume providing services again.

I certainly remember the couple who lamented that their teenage girls aged 13 and 15 years did not help at all around the house. Worse still, the parents were devastated at the way that the girls spoke to them, behaved towards them and swore at them.

On further inquiry, the parents said that they did all that they could for their girls in that they gave them the best of everything, sent them to a private school, took them on overseas holidays, and gave them the latest designer label clothes.

When the eldest went out on Saturday night for example, the father said that he would press $50 into her hand and tell her to have a good night.

My response was to ask whether I could come and live at their place too and be part of all the goodies and treats!

---

13. Make adolescents responsible for their actions.

If your adolescent has not done their homework, don't be tempted to write an excuse in her school diary to get her off the hook. If he has left his lunch at home or has left his gym or sports clothes at home, you don't need to be running half way across town to drop in his goods to school and thereby also messing up your own day and program.

"At every step the child should be allowed to meet the real experiences of life; the thorns should never be plucked from his roses."

(Ellen Key; 1849-1926, Swedish Writer)

Adolescents need to understand that their actions bring about certain natural or logical consequences. That is how they learn about reality. You do not need to punish them yourself if there is an automatic consequence. Your punishment only teaches them unpleasant things about you.

One adolescent whom I saw used to be relatively disorganized in the mornings getting ready for school.

She usually got up late and had to be called a number of times. After a quick shower, she ate a piece of toast quickly for breakfast (if she ever had time for breakfast) usually standing up at the kitchen bench and then in a scurry tried to pack her school bag trying to remember what lessons she had on for the day. She pulled on her shoes as she headed out the door for the school bus.

If she happened to miss the bus, she would turn around, go back home and tell her mother to take her to school. The mother always did, but complained bitterly to me that her daughter was rarely if ever organized in the mornings and that it was a hectic rush and almost chaos.

I suggested that the mother sit down calmly with her daughter and explain that from this point onward, she would **not** run her daughter to school because she had her own life to lead and did not want to have to frequently rearrange her own schedule due to the daughter's lack of organization.

The daughter would either have to wait for the next bus and be late for school and take the penalty or catch a taxi and pay for it out of her own money, but the mother would no longer be the chauffeur.

The mother also rang the school and advised the Year Coordinator of the "new" plan and that if the daughter happened to be late, that the mother expected that there would be an appropriate penalty delivered.

Indeed, the daughter managed to be on time for the school bus for three consecutive weeks which was a record.

In the fourth week, she missed the bus. Mother stood by her word and there was no ride to school. The daughter was late and had to do the punishment.

She never missed another bus for that year.

14. Don't sweat the issues of style.

We know that we all have different ways of doing things.

Perhaps as a parent you might not have considered that there were alternative ways of doing something or perhaps your way was the 'perfect' way. Irrespective, don't let the little things irritate you; it's simply not worth it.

One of my sons, when he was little, used to like to get dressed in bed in the morning because it was warmer in there.

It used to drive me crazy. I had a thousand good reasons why he should get dressed outside of his bed during the winter-time. But he was always ready on time to go to school and organized when it was time to leave. Ultimately, I had to learn to let him get out of bed in his unique way without making it a moral issue.

Incidentally, it only lasted for about 18 months when he was in preparatory school.

It is highly probable, if not certain, that your adolescent will choose a different style of dress, want different entertainment and use different language. These are only matters of style.

As a parent, you need to keep your perspective. These are not world shattering issues. The world will not end because your adolescent wants to do it differently.

"Teenagers express a burning desire to be different from anyone else, but then dress exactly alike."

(Author Unknown)

Your adolescent will also listen to a different type of music. You can't be expected to live with it, like it or embrace it in any way.

In fact, their music may down right offend you. It tends to flake the paint, lift the wall tiles, and undermine the house foundations as well as erupt your eardrums and play havoc with your sinuses.

"The young always have the same problem – how to rebel and conform at the same time. They have now solved this by defying their parents and copying one another."

(Quentin Crisp; 1908-1999, English Writer)

The lyrics though, help you to better understand what's relevant to teenagers, how scary it is to be an adolescent and the messages with which they are being bombarded.

Remember too what your parents once said about Elvis Presley not to mention "The Beatles," "The Rolling Stones," "Led Zeppelin" and "Cold Chisel!"

15. Don't allow your adolescent to have total "time-out."

Some adolescents shut themselves away in a self-imposed time-out usually in their own rooms. Typically, they play computer games, listen to heavy metal rock music, or "veg out."

Of course, it is important to respect one another's privacy, but when adolescents have a life of almost total isolation, this is not good for them or for you. Don't let them hide in their rooms and keep their lives a secret from you.

If requests to join the family don't work or incentives such as dollars to work for a friend of yours don't work, then you may need to take more radical steps to really break the pattern or cycle that your adolescent is into.

See for example, if you can arrange for your teenager to visit his uncle in a northern city for a period or perhaps stay with his auntie out west on her farm.

The aim is to break the pattern.

16. There are two main areas you need to monitor with your adolescent; their time and their money.

Whenever parents cannot account for what their adolescent is doing with either their time or their money, there are generally problems that arise.

Experience shows that clinically, whenever an adolescent has been referred to me for drug-taking, without exception, the parents have lost touch with what their teen is doing with his or her time and/or money.

Keep track of both.   Keep track of what your adolescent is doing.

A father called frantically to say that his 14-year-old son in 9th Grade had just been expelled from a private school for smoking marijuana in the classroom and could I help. I saw the son and parents next day and the son confided that he had been trying marijuana for a few years now. He said it was easy in that his parents did not suspect him in any way and he would lie about where he was and with whom.

He used to also sell pirated CDs to get some money for the drugs. His parents never knew about how much money he had or where he spent it. He also knew that he hung around with the "wrong crowd" both in and out of school, but said that his parents never really showed much concern about this, apparently believing that it was "just adolescence."

---

17. If there are two or more parents, you mustn't undercut or sabotage one another, and you mustn't fight it out in front of the adolescent.

As parents, you don't have to be right, but you do have to be together. Otherwise, the adolescent will divide and conquer. He or she will drive a wedge between you.

It's human nature to want to "win" or "score points," and one sure-fire way of doing this is to undermine or divide the opposition. As children, we may have tried it too with our parents – it may not have worked, but that doesn't mean we didn't try it.

As parents, it is important to get your act together and present as a team. Anything less and the family unit starts to disintegrate.

United we stand, divided we fall.

Sam's parents complained that they could not seem to agree on how to manage their son. They seemed to be able to communicate fine when he wasn't around, but most of their arguments were over him.

I asked if they would mind if I could see Sam alone in my office while they waited in the waiting room. I had a hunch. I told Sam that I figured that he was a smart boy and that he was a good people reader and that no doubt he'd worked out how to manage mom and dad. Sam smiled and looked kind of smug and proud.

He said that he could almost always get what he wanted; dad was the "hard" one of the two parents and mum was the "soft" one. His technique was to see his father first and generally get a "no" response and then he'd go plead his case to his mother who would usually say "yes." From that point, he said that mom and dad would usually have an argument; they'd give up in despair and he would get what he wanted.

This young man was learning how to be very manipulative and he was winning!

18. Don't let your teenagers embarrass you.

Don't let the reactions of frantic friends, staring strangers, righteous relatives or indignant instructors be more important than the feelings of your adolescent who just made a humiliating mess or public stuff-up.

This is the time they need you to stand by them, not ridicule them, rouse on them or add to their embarrassment.

They need your support, not your added condemnation – if they can't rely on you in their hour of need, who can they rely on?

19. Practice short-term memory loss.

Refuse to recall what they did wrong the day before. Pretend that you have a memory deficit (which some of us have already as we get older!). Start each day as if it were a new relationship. Don't keep score.

Adolescents change so very rapidly and self-consciously. Most days it will be a new start and a new day and a "new" adolescent!

20. Whatever age your teenagers, try to give them a hug every day.

Certainly, in this day and age, like never before, where we have the internet, iPods, mobile phones, and high-tech, we need "high-touch."

It has been suggested that we need a minimum of

four hugs a day for emotional and personal health. No doubt, four would be over the top for some adolescents, but definitely try for one even though they might protest about it.

Don't give in – remember, you're supposed to be "weird" anyway.

21.   Don't have a nervous breakdown about what your adolescent is doing (or not doing) until you have discussed it with a psychologist.

Sometimes it is critical to get an independent opinion.

Talk with someone who is not biased, who is not emotionally involved and hopefully, someone who has had some expert training in the field.

You may need a psychologist unless you have had training in parenting yourselves, are a particularly cooperative and harmonious couple, or are supported by a good team of aunts and uncles, grandparents or extended family.

22. Keep in touch with their academic performances.

You need to know how your adolescent is going at school. You need to keep in touch.

If they are doing well and their grades are fine, reward them and tell them how proud you are of their achievements. If you are getting notes in their diary or negative reports on their Term or Semester reports, you need to explore further with the school as to what they perceive is occurring. You need to know what is happening in all aspects of your adolescent's life.

So many parents see me at the end of the year or semester frustrated that the school report has been so negative for their son or daughter and that the poor behavior such as not handing up work and missing deadlines for example, has been occurring for some weeks and maybe throughout the whole term.

"Why weren't we told before this?" they ask me. True. But why didn't they ask and why didn't they keep in touch. Why did they wait for the report? It works both ways.

---

23. As a last resort, call the police.

If your adolescent is doing something that is against the law such as stealing from home or being violent and damaging property, then, the police need to be involved.

Teenagers must understand that the world supports your efforts to raise them. Your adolescent must understand that there are logical consequences for illegal behavior.

Of course, if you too are being violent or abusive to your teenager or property, then that really is being a foolhardy parent (and person). You must model appropriate behavior in the first place.

24. Catch your teenager being "good."

How often do you really praise your adolescent?

No, not just when they happen to get an "A" grade in Legal Studies or Art or Maths or throw the winning goal in netball or kick the winning goal in football or whatever. I mean, praise them for all **the little things** that they do.

I've never yet met an adolescent who is 100% bad 100% of the time. The way that some parents talk and act though, you'd believe that their child was from outer space and **never ever** did anything right. This is completely discouraging for parents and teenagers alike.

What about getting to school on time, coming to the table when asked, handing up pieces of work on time, being sociable and communicative, doing regular work-outs in the gym, ironing their shirts, keeping the volume on the TV down low and so on?

Catch your adolescent being good and you may well get some pleasant surprises.

25. If older teenagers want to leave home, let them leave.

Some parents are petrified that their son/daughter is going to leave home. They have to one day anyway, you know.

If they do decide to leave home and they get along all right without you, then they were right – they didn't need you after all. It's critically important that they become independent and find their own survival techniques – remember that this is part of finding one's identity.

However, if you're not too unpleasant and mean, they may see that they are not ready yet to go it alone, and they may want to return home; then that's probably better for you both.

Either way it's win-win.

26.   Remind your adolescent that mistakes are learning experiences.

We have been wrongly taught that mistakes are awful and that we can't afford to make any. Unfortunately, our education system too reinforces this notion.

Worse still, we have been taught that if we do happen to muck up somehow, that we as individuals, as persons, are absolutely hopeless or dumb or stupid.

"The biggest myth in education and life is that somehow, we're not allowed to make mistakes – yet making mistakes is the basis for learning."

(Darryl Cross)

Somehow or other, we have also been led to believe that rather than our particular **actions or behavior** being a problem and needing to be rectified, we blame ourselves.

Instead, we need to make sure that very early in life our children and our adolescents understand quite clearly that *"mistakes are negative outcomes leading to success."* In other words, mistakes need to be seen as things we do that help us to refine our behavior, actions and thoughts.

Mistakes are only a problem if we keep making the same one and not learning from it!

Anyone who has ever achieved has made lots of mistakes. Anyone who has been successful will tell you that they made mistakes, but learned from them. I have talked to many leaders and achievers and without exception, they readily admit that they made mistakes, but learnt the lesson and moved on. Mistakes are what we learn from, to self-correct, to get back on target again or change course to take advantage of our new learning.

"Mistakes are negative outcomes leading to success."

(Author Unknown)

Mistakes are not an excuse to give up, to beat up on ourselves about how dumb we are, to tell ourselves that we're hopeless or that we'll never make it. This is such rubbish, but I hear it constantly from teenagers. In fact, my clinical experience shows me quite clearly that the number one problem we have in our general community, and especially with our adolescents is that we feel not good enough or "inferior."

Generally, the issue of making mistakes or being afraid to make mistakes creates **two types of teenagers; the anxious and the depressed.**

(1) There is the teenager who becomes paralyzed to move or act. They **fear** goofing up somehow. They say to me things such as "*what if....*" and they become very anxious about putting their hand up in class, about speaking out, about suggesting anything, about engaging others in conversation, and about saying hello to the opposite sex. They are afraid to try anything.

(2) There is the teenager who worries constantly about what he or she says or does. They sometimes refer to themselves as "worry warts" and they tend to become **depressed** about what they have said or done or not said or not done. Unfortunately, they often try to compensate by striving to be perfect in all that they do which is a no-win street.

Taken to an extreme, these adolescents sometimes don't start assignments, essays or projects for fear of failing or making a mistake. They are concerned that somehow or other, they won't do a good job or get it right. The shame, embarrassment, guilt or anxiety would be too overwhelming for them and too painful. They become trapped in their fear.

They say things to me that start with "If only...." (e.g. "if only I hadn't said that," "if only I hadn't gone to the party," "if only I had more personality"). Alternatively, they say things to me that start with "I wish...." (e.g. "I wish I was more friendly and talkative," "I wish I didn't worry so much," "I wish I was happier").

They become overwhelmed by their darkness, their failures and their so-called incompetence. The answer to this lies in them firstly, not only wanting to change, but secondly, in how they view mistakes and in re-programming how they talk to themselves.

27. Don't lose your sense of humor.

It is tempting to get intense, be serious and carry on as though you are in a court of law. While it is true that some things do demand a certain intensity, in the main, remember to laugh. It has been said that parents who laugh, last the distance.

Try to be light-hearted as much as possible. It helps the communication and it helps the level of tension in a household. That doesn't mean you need to be sarcastic or delve into put downs which is just a poor attempt at humor at the other person's expense. Instead, it means seeing the funny side of things, lightening up and sometimes laughing at yourself too!

28. If you are a single parent......

(a) ....a single mother of a teenage son, don't let your son think he is the boss.

If you are the natural mother, it is your duty to discipline, guide and control your son. You need to accept your authority. Pulling in a male partner to help with parenting and running the house is setting it up for guerrilla warfare. Don't try to bring in a new stepfather unless he is extraordinarily humble and powerless. If he is not "powerless," there will be ugly battles and the partner will eventually leave anyhow.

If you feel the need for a male partner in parenting, contact the real father, or perhaps an uncle or grandfather, but you stay in charge.

(b) ....a single mother of a teenage son, don't lean on the son and make him the "husband" or "father."

As a mother, you are the adult. Don't distort the family boundaries by looking for a partner in your son, someone to confide in and talk to, and someone who can share in the running of the house. Also, don't try to bring your son on-side against your former husband to form an alliance. You'll only serve to throw things out of balance.

Let teenagers be teenagers. He will become a husband or partner or father in his own time. Trying to fulfill your needs through your son only serves to prevent him from finding his real identity. It might serve a purpose for you in the short-term, but it only serves to undermine your adolescent's development.

(c) ....a single mother of a teenage daughter, don't lean on the daughter and make her the "friend" and "confidante."

Again, you are the mother, not the friend. Your daughter has friends; she does not need to have you in that category as well.

Confiding in your daughter only puts her in a bind about her responsibilities to her natural father and how she responds to him. It puts her in a bind about how she should act and be. It simply confuses her and complicates life for her. Don't do it.

Go out and find yourself another friend who can support you and in whom you can confide.

(d) ....a single father of a teenage son, don't try to be the male buck taking on the young buck.

Trying to dominate the young buck never works. It normally leads to verbal abuse of each other and then finally, physical abuse.

Of course, once it gets to that stage, the relationship has deteriorated almost irretrievably.

Instead, you as the father are the adult. Act like one.

Don't let your ego get in the way and don't pretend that you can carry on at home like you do at work where you can boss everyone around. You're at home and your son needs you – as a model and as a parent.

You talk things out rationally and if that doesn't work, you go the calm, quiet routine (but firm) and generally that confuses the heck out of him.

(e) ....a single father of a teenage daughter, don't put the daughter up as a substitute wife or partner.

Your daughter is after-all, your daughter, not a partner. Don't confuse her by treating her like an equal – she is not.

It is important for her own development that she remains a daughter and is able to find herself and her identity in her own time without blurring the boundaries and throwing her off track.

If you need a partner, find one yourself, but make sure that your daughter still has pride of place in your life and does not all of a sudden play second fiddle to the new partner in your life. You daughter needs you, but not as a partner.

29. Teach your teenager that there is a mind, body, heart...& spirit.

Psychology in the main has been very helpful in allowing us to understand ourselves, but in the same breath, it has done us a disservice by generally omitting a significant portion of who we are as individuals. We are made up of four parts as shown below.

The tide in psychology seems to be turning as books like those by Ken Wilbur titled *"Integral Psychology"* point us again to the notion that there is certainly more to us, for example, than just our minds and our bodies.

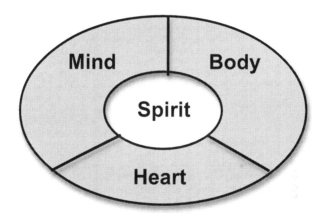

The World Health Organization has predicted that by the year 2020, 1 in 5 of our adolescents will be suffering from depression. Various writers have suggested that we will have an "epidemic" on our hands.

I do not want to suggest, however, that the main feature in contributing to this apparent epidemic is the failure to recognize our spiritual dimension. Nevertheless, I observe that those adolescents who acknowledge that there is another dimension called their spirit and that this dimension needs to be recognized and exercised, like we exercise our minds and bodies, seem to cope better overall.

This spiritual dimension is often exercised through meditation, through prayer, and through quiet daily reflection and reading. Most adolescents (and adults too), on the other hand, want to plug their day with noise, busyness and activity.

Instead, the spiritual component is generally an individual experience which requires quiet, peace and stillness. It's amazing what comes to us out of the stillness – if we dare to stop and listen.

Some adolescents share their spiritual awareness through attending church or youth groups and camps and this, of course, is encouraged because it also means that they are learning to socialize, interact and communicate in yet another setting beyond school and family.

It is often out of this spiritual awareness that adolescents find their mission in life, their purpose and their goal.

The spiritual dimension cannot be underestimated.

30. Aim to give your adolescents two things: roots & wings.

Your aim is to give your adolescent a strong foundation based on love and moral values that essentially is rooted in the family's way of life.

These characteristics, values and perspectives give them the courage and ability to fly like eagles and leave the family nest in order to wing it independently on their own.

"I have found that the best way to give advice to your children is to find out what they want and then advise them to do it."

(Harry S Truman; 1884-1972, 33rd President of the United States)

CHAPTER 6 SUMMARY

What are some really important tips that help us to be better parents?

1. **Stay linked to your adolescent.**

2. **Learn to listen, really listen.**

3. **Keep adolescents on the move.**

4. **Make the rules crystal clear.**

5. **Be unshockable.**

6. **Don't "up" any punishment as a way of trying to get on top of your adolescent.**

7. **Don't assume that physical growth = emotional growth.**

8. **Be up-front about puberty.**

9. **Guarantee complete confidentiality.**

10. **Don't expect perfect compliance.**

11. **Forget the "When I was your age…"**

12. **If teenagers flatly refuse to cooperate, refuse to provide goods and services for them.**

13. **Make adolescents responsible for their actions.**

14. **Don't sweat the issues of style.**

15. Don't allow your adolescent to have total "time-out."

16. There are two main areas you need to monitor with your adolescent; their time and their money.

17. If there are two or more parents, you mustn't undercut or sabotage one another, and you mustn't fight it out in front of the adolescent.

18. Don't let your teenagers embarrass you.

19. Practice short-term memory loss.

20. Whatever age your teenager, try to give them a hug every day.

21. Don't have a nervous breakdown about what your adolescent is doing (or not doing) until you have discussed it with a psychologist.

22. Keep in touch with their academic performances.

23. As a last resort, call the police.

24. Catch your teenager being "good".

25. If older teenagers want to leave home, let them leave.

26. Remind your adolescent that mistakes are learning experiences.

27. Don't lose your sense of humor.

28. If you are a single parent……
     (a) …. a single mother of a teenage son, don't let your son think he is the boss.
     (b) …. a single mother of a teenage son, don't lean on the son and make him the "husband" or "father."
     (c) …. a single mother of a teenage daughter, don't lean on the daughter and make her the "friend" and "confidante."
     (d) …. a single father of a teenage son, don't try to be the male buck taking on the young buck.
     (e) …. a single father of a teenage daughter, don't put the daughter up as a substitute wife or partner.

29. Teach your teenager that there is a mind, body, heart… & spirit.

30. Aim to give your adolescents two things: roots & wings.

CHAPTER 7

Frequently Asked Questions

These are some of the most common questions that I have been asked over a couple of decades or more of private clinical practice as well as giving presentations to various kindergartens and pre-schools together with primary, preparatory, high school and secondary schools including teaching staff and parents and friends groups.

1. What do you do in a situation where an adolescent or teenager who is obviously upset, refuses to communicate, but is quite rude in their mannerisms and responses to our advances as parents?

First and most important, there is no point in reacting angrily. It is certainly natural for parents to want to yell and scream and blow their top. However, the issue has to be addressed in another way. Don't be confrontational. If the adolescent is already "off-side" there is little point going in as a parent with guns drawn ready for a showdown at high noon.

Instead, approach your teenager with a calm exterior (inside though, you may be ready to lynch the teenager). Don't be accusatory or ask intrusive questions because this will only turn off your adolescent and get him or her on the defensive.

Follow the formula along these lines:

- say in your **calm** tones how you are feeling (e.g. "I'm really at a loss to know what you want and it hurts that you are abrupt and blunt with me").
- **listen for their response** and if they grunt something back at you, don't go into defense mode yourself, but paraphrase what you heard them say (e.g. "I get the sense that you don't want to talk to me right now or that somehow I'm an interference, is that right?") Try very hard to understand their position.
- **at some point, you will need to add that you are not prepared for this kind of "treatment" to continue** (e.g. "I'm not prepared for you to go on speaking to me in this manner and if you continue to talk to me in this way, then I don't see why I should continue to prepare meals and generally look after you.")

Remember, say this in quiet, calm tones.

2. Should adolescents receive pocket money and if so, how much is enough?

Two things are certain: first, as far as the adolescent is concerned, it will never be enough! Secondly, the teenager is sure to mount a case to try to argue or manipulate for more money because "all my friends get $50 a week and here I am, I get nothing and you parents are really mean."

The aim of pocket money is to teach the adolescent how to use and value money appropriately. In other words, it is about trying to get them to understand that there is a finite amount of money and as such, they have to apportion out how they will use that cash and use it wisely.

The amounts may vary depending on what the pocket money is used for. If it includes travel to school, bus or train fares, as well as lunch money, then $25-$30 per week may well be appropriate. If it is only for general entertainment (e.g. movies, fun parlors, outings), food (e.g. hamburgers, thick shakes, smoothies, sweets), then $10-$15 may be more appropriate.

At the end of the day, no matter what your decision, stick by it and don't be conned by all the stories or hard luck tales that you might hear about how the pocket money or allowance is a pittance and needs to be raised.

One further point. Pocket money can also certainly be tied to the adolescent doing their daily or weekly chores such as feeding the dog, putting out the garbage, bringing in the wood for the fire, keeping their room clean and so forth. This is especially so if pocket money is really only for entertainment and recreational purposes – no chores, no money.

"There's nothing wrong with the younger generation that becoming taxpayers won't cure."

(Dan Bennett; US Comedian)

3. How do you know if your teen is on drugs?

Some parents who have come to me for counsel have been shocked that they did not see any of the signs of their adolescent being on drugs. They are bewildered, confused and angry that they somehow missed it and that their son or daughter deceived, lied or manipulated them.

Typically, there are **some telltale signs** such as the following:
- Wild mood swings and explosive outbursts
- Excessive tiredness and inability to concentrate in school
- Staying out all night
- Trouble with the police
- Trouble at school
- Sudden change of friends
- Unexplained need for more money
- Withdrawal or staying in their room

Of course, it's true that many young people show these signs as a natural part of growing up. However, if they continue to behave strangely or differently, there could well be a problem.

You also need to realize that there are **three main types of drugs** including:

(1) Depressants including cannabis (marijuana), tranquillizers, heroine, morphine, opium, methadone and most inhalants (alcohol is also a depressant),
(2) Stimulants including amphetamines (speed) and cocaine (nicotine and caffeine are also mild stimulants),
(3) Hallucinogens including LSD and magic mushrooms.

Cannabis is the most widely used illegal drug in western countries including Australia. Cannabis is illegal, but drug laws in Australia for example, distinguish between those who use drugs and those who supply or traffic drugs. There are three main forms of cannabis including marijuana, hashish and hash oil. *Marijuana, however, is the most common and least powerful form of cannabis.*

The active chemical in cannabis and therefore marijuana is THC (Delta-9 tetrahydrocannabinol), which affects the central nervous system and slows down the messages going to and from the brain to the body. Cannabis is therefore classified as a depressant drug although it can also have mild hallucinogenic effects. When people are affected by marijuana they are said to be "stoned", "bent" or "high." Traces of THC can remain detectable in urine samples for days, even perhaps weeks, after use. It is absorbed into the bloodstream through the walls of the lungs if it is smoked or through the walls of the stomach and intestines if it is eaten.

The most recent survey reported from the late 1990's (Centre for Behavioral Research in Cancer, Anti-cancer Council of Victoria, November, 1998) indicated that 36% of all secondary students aged between 12 and 17 years reported the use of cannabis at some time in their life. Cannabis use increased with age from 13% of 12-year-olds to 55% of 17-year-olds. Weekly use also increased with age from 3% of 12-year-olds to 16% of 17-year-olds. Weekly use was also more common amongst boys than girls.

The **immediate effects of marijuana** which last two to three hours after smoking include the following:

• **Relaxation and loss of inhibition** (the person feels

happy, relaxed, comfortable and they may feel less inhibited and friendly and laugh spontaneously; some people become quiet and reflective and some may become sleepy)

- **Increased appetite** (this usually includes snacking on junk food)
- **Affected perception** (increased awareness and the perception of color, sound and other sensations; it can also affect vision and perception of time and space)
- **Poor coordination** (reduced coordination and balance making it dangerous to drive or operate machinery)
- **Thinking and memory** (impact on memory and the ability to think logically and people can lose track of what they are saying or thinking; some people may imagine that they have also had profound ideas or insights)
- **Other** (increased heart rate, low blood pressure, faintness, reddened eyes, and a "hangover" effect like drowsiness and poor coordination which can last for several hours beyond the initial effects)

The **long-term effects of marijuana** use include the following:

- **Respiratory illness** (including lung cancer and chronic bronchitis)
- **Decreased motivation** (including less energy and a lack of motivation so that performance at school or work suffers)
- **Brain dysfunction** (concentration, and memory and the ability to learn are all reduced)
- **Impact on hormones** (hormone production is affected including a lower sex drive, irregular menstrual cycles and lowered sperm counts)
- **Induced psychosis** (this is characterized by

hallucinations, delusions, memory loss and confusion including episodes of schizophrenia or manic depressive psychosis especially among those who are vulnerable because of a personal or family history of mental illness)

A parent's worst fear is that their adolescent may turn to drugs or may be on drugs, but it is important to remember that while many adolescents may experiment with the drug initially, the percentage that use it regularly on a weekly basis is small.

Nevertheless, it is important for parents to be informed about drugs especially marijuana so that they can try to deal with it in a calm, rational manner rather than become too hysterical and out of control if their adolescent was caught using marijuana.

In most major cities or towns, there is an Alcohol and Drug Information Service and the following web sites could also be very helpful:

www.adf.org.au
www.theantidrug.com/drug_info/
www.drugabuse.gov/drugpages.html
www.drugs-info.co.uk/
www.thesite.org/drinkanddrugs

"There is no magic decoding ring that will help us read our adolescent's feelings. Rather, what we need to do is hold out our antennae in the hope that we'll pick up the right signals."

(The Lions Clubs International)

4. What can you do about the influence of the peer group because the adolescent's friends seem to have more sway over the adolescent than their parents do?

Parents are naturally concerned about the kinds of friends their children choose, since friends may counteract parental influence.

"Most literature on the culture of adolescence focuses on peer pressure as a negative force. Warnings about the 'wrong crowd' read like tornado alerts in parent manuals....It is a relative term that means different things in different places. In Fort Wayne, for example, the wrong crowd meant hanging out with liberal Democrats. In Connecticut, it meant kids who weren't planning to get a Ph.D. from Yale."

(Mary Kay Blakely; US Journalist & author)

Children belong to two worlds: the world of adults and that of their peers. This is particularly so as they approach their teen years. Parents rightly concern themselves more, at this stage, about the "good" and "bad" influences in their children's lives. They worry about the company they keep, as they grow out of, and away from, the family.

• one group can foster hostile, disobedient, uncreative individuals;

- another can develop confused, purposeless drifters;
- and still another can produce co-operative, flexible, purposeful, altruistic children.

In turn, the atmosphere of the group is determined by the qualities of its leaders and those of the other group members.

Research Tips

Research into adolescence demonstrates:

1) the importance of keeping track of what children are doing; i.e. *keep track of how they spend their time and money.*
2) that the tendency to conform to the group, especially a same sex group, *increases during the early part of adolescence, peaking around 13 to 16 years, and then waning.* This may be a relief for some parents. It often seems that all the good work you thought you were putting into raising your children is being swept away by the influence of their peer group. You may be pleased to hear that your children will grow past that peak of group conformity and start to think for themselves again. Usually your influence shows itself again at that point.

Peer Influence

The influence of the peer group may be widespread, as in clothing fashions and entertainment choices (with some help from the marketers), or localised, as in approving certain types of behaviour, for better or worse. For example, the peer group is the strongest influence, after parental example, in determining whether adolescents smoke or not. Don't overreact to the influence of peers on your adolescent.

On many issues, the peer group's values will be similar to yours because adolescents tend to pick friends from similar family backgrounds to their own. The group's values are most likely to differ from yours in choice of dress, music and entertainment, expectations about dating, and use of language. If you think about it, you will realise that these are mostly obvious issues. They can loom large, but they are not necessarily very important.

Peers a dominating influence?

When the peer group does seem to be playing a very dominant role in an adolescent's life, this sometimes reflects a lack of attention from, and poor relationships with parents.

Adolescents who are very strongly peer-orientated are more likely to hold negative views of themselves and of their friends, and to report less affection, support and discipline at home. In contrast, an adolescent with good self-confidence will be more able to choose his or her own values, independently of the peer group, a choice that is the essence of finding their own identity.

Therefore, if peer group influence seems to be a problem, the real problem probably lies much closer to home, and that's where the solution may need to be found, too.

5. How do you make adolescents responsible?

More often than not, one of the major problems – if not the **major issue** – parents have with their teenagers concerns the issue of **responsibility**.

Most of the time parents realize that their long-term goal is to raise independent, responsible young adults.

Unfortunately, parents often behave as if the way to create responsible young adults is to nag, remind, coerce, threaten and punish them until they are 18 years old or so then suddenly, set them free – and somehow or other, they will then automatically be independent and responsible!

Like any complex behavior, responsibility must be learned over time.

For example, by the age of 12, the pre-adolescent should be entirely accountable for his or her schoolwork. The parent is accountable for providing a desk or table, a chair, light, paper, and pencil, and for offering assistance when needed, but the child is accountable for the actual work.

The logical consequence for not doing homework is obvious – poor grades, repeating the year, having to do remedial work, or possibly even dropping out.   The "school of hard knocks" can be an excellent teacher – far more effective than parental nagging.   Helping your teenager set personal goals can however, help them avoid these extremes.

Why does a proportion of first year University students fail or drop out?   Once they become tertiary students and are largely left on their own, they have not learned how to be independent and how to handle their new found time and freedom; therefore they fail.

Most parents complain that their teenagers are **not** responsible for their household chores, school homework, and many other obligations.   Typically, parents react to the situation by nagging their adolescent to be responsible, harshly criticizing their irresponsible behavior, and punishing them.

Such tactics rarely are effective for any of us let alone teens.   Any teenager though who is being nagged, criticized, or punished for irresponsible behavior is highly unlikely to strive to become more responsible.   Instead, the teenager will become angry.

An angry teenager will either:

- become depressed and withdraw or isolate him or herself,
- be angry and act out in obvious ways,
- be passive-aggressive in manner and retaliate in an indirect, manipulative fashion designed to sabotage.

Most irresponsible teenagers express their displeasure with their parents by continuing to be irresponsible. They rarely become responsible when coerced.

As parents, ask yourself honestly, "How did you learn to be responsible?" Most say, "It happened over time." Most reasonable, responsible adults learn to be generally responsible through living awhile and experiencing logical consequences.

What therefore is the model to use to teach our adolescent to be responsible?

1) Identify specific tasks that need to be done and goals that need to be met.
2) Make sure that the teenager understands what those tasks/goals are and either have them written down or be clearly discussed.
3) Give the teenager the time and the opportunity to choose to meet those goals.
4) Reinforce the teenager for behaving responsibly.
5) If the teenager chooses irresponsibly, ignore that poor behavior and allow the logical consequence to happen.
6) If deemed necessary, apply a specific consequence to the teenager for a specific, seriously irresponsible behavior.

In this manner, the parent no longer has the burden of *making* the adolescent behave responsibly; the parent simply identifies goals and rewards, ignores, or at times provides a consequence when the adolescent makes a bad behavior choice. The parent is now off the hook. The parent is no longer the policeman.

The teenager is "on the hook" to be responsible or not. Either way, the teenager will learn – just the way most of us adults did.

6. How do you make teenagers do their chores?

When parents ask their adolescent to do a task or a chore, recognize that the adolescent is somewhat obligated; he or she owes something (in the form of a deed) to the parent. If the teenager does the task that you asked to be done, make sure that you say thank you and that you appreciate it being done (but don't let it go unnoticed!).

As we all know so very well, many teenagers will procrastinate or perhaps argue when given a chore. What is a parent then most likely to do? The parent typically proceeds to yell, scream, threaten, demean, or coerce. The teenager now, or course, feels angry. In fact, any "debt" he or she felt might have been owed to the parent is now cancelled out.

While the adolescent might have felt slightly obligated when first asked to do something by the parents, after being screamed at and criticized harshly, the teenager then feels he or she has more than paid the debt; there is little or no remorse at all for not fulfilling the parent's request.

The parent, in this situation, has simply "made the adolescent get even."

Instead, ask the adolescent calmly to do a specific task. Do not argue and do not stand there and insist that the job get done instantly -- unless it is absolutely mandatory that it be done immediately.

Understand that the task may get done, but not in "your time." It may be after the teenager has done whatever they wanted to do such as watch a TV program. Let the weight of the request or obligation rest on the adolescent. While this tactic certainly does not guarantee that the teenager will be responsible, it at least assures that the parents do not provide the teenager with a handy excuse not to do the chores.

It also needs to be said quite clearly, that we live by our habits.

So, make your job as a parent easier by setting up routines early about what jobs need to be done when. "Early" means when they are younger in primary or preparatory grades or "early" means as they start to hit puberty. Don't try to implement routines when the adolescent is aged 15-years or more; it's too hard. Not impossible, but more difficult.

For example, sit down and establish expectations about appropriate hygiene and self-care and what is expected about the state of their bedroom. Then put in place routines that seek to make these expectations come true. Before school, the bedroom needs to be left in a tidy state and the pets fed. After school, the uniform needs to be removed and the lunchbox put on the kitchen bench and so on.

For further tips on teenagers doing their chores, see the comments above on how to make your teenager "responsible."

7. Should a teenager be punished and if so, what is appropriate?

Adolescents tend to become resentful – and revengeful – when punishment is applied. Therefore, punishment needs to be used sparingly with teenagers and when it is used, it must be administered appropriately.

You use punishment because you want to:

- **alert** the teenager that some behavior is unacceptable
- **stop** that poor behavior
- attempt to **ensure** that the poor behavior does not occur again.

You can only accomplish this if you, as the parent, generally **remain calm** while administering the punishment. Screaming and yelling at an adolescent will most likely receive ranting and raving in return; little positive benefit will result from such interaction.

If the parent becomes excessively angry, the adolescent responds to the parent's emotion and **not** to the resulting penalty. *The message gets lost in the medium.* The punishment, therefore, becomes ineffective.

Remember that punishment is **not** revenge or retribution. It is not a basic tenet of punishment theory to make the teenager at least as upset as is the parent!

Besides, most teenagers will not give the parents the satisfaction of letting them know that the punishment "got to them!" Don't expect that they'll show that it affected them.

So, what are the rules of punishment?

1) **Be calm and matter-of-fact** to allow the goals of punishment to remain in focus.

2) **Punish immediately.** The closer the connection between the punishment and the poor behavior, the more effective the punishment.

3) **Be specific.** The teenager must understand clearly and specifically what he or she did that was wrong (for example, it is difficult to correct or punish a "bad attitude" or "being lazy" – whatever they are).

4) **Be able to enforce the punishment.** Many parents apply punishments that they cannot realistically enforce or make stick e.g. banning television after school when the parent is not there to enforce it.

5) **Keep the punishment brief.** For young children, punishments should last no longer than the remainder of the day. With teenagers, most punishments should probably last no more than through the following weekend or for, at most, a week or two. If a teenager is punished for too long for a misdemeanor or is made to become too upset, the teenager stops thinking about his or her misdeed and simply becomes angry. The adolescent is then more likely to think about ways to get even than about the irresponsible behavior.

In essence, a sound formula for expressing your displeasure at something that your adolescent has done involves the following 2 aspects:

(1)   **Give an "I" – Message.** In assertiveness training, for instance, individuals are taught to clearly express their feelings without resorting to accusations, criticisms and

yelling. This concept is often referred to as an *"I-message."* For example, "I really resent it when you leave your sneakers in the hallway where it looks untidy and people can trip over them, so from now on I'd like you to take them off in your room and put them away in your cupboard."

Telling a teenager what one *sees* or *hears* and how one *feels* can lead to a behavior change. Unlike a child, an adolescent needs to save face and probably will wait a bit – possibly a day or two – before changing the behavior. It is difficult, but parents need to be patient!

At the very least, with an I-message, the parent clearly communicates to the teenager how he or she feels about a particular misbehavior.

(2)   **Give Consequences.** Penalizing an adolescent for a particular inappropriate behavior is technically defined as "applying consequences." When handing out a consequence, the parent must keep in mind all the guidelines already discussed above i.e. react in low key manner, be specific about the misdeed, make the penalty brief, and be sure the punishment is enforceable.

Some penalties parents typically can enforce are:

- withholding allowances or pocket money,
- removal of the phone in the teenager's room,
- putting a lock on the phone,
- removal of the hi-fi system from the teenager's room,
- changing the password on the home computer,
- removing the internet from the computer in the teen's room,
- removal of the television from the teenager's room,
- confiscating the Nintendo module or play-station,
- locking the doors if the teenager leaves

inappropriately or is past curfew,
- un-inviting the teenager to a family outing or a trip,
- refusing to pay car petrol,
- calling the police if the teenager takes the car without permission.

With **children**, punishment is used primarily to discontinue inappropriate behavior. With **adolescents**, punishment is unlikely to significantly alter behavior, but it generally sends a clear signal that a particular misbehavior is not acceptable.

8. Should we smack or spank our kids?

A note on that continual topic of corporal punishment.

Corporal punishment with teenagers is ineffective. Hitting or smacking teenagers squashes their self-esteem, makes them terribly angry, and most importantly, loses the focus on the misdeed that they committed.

Remember, your teenager might be as strong as you, or sooner or later might be stronger than you. One thing will lead to another and experience shows that you may well end up hitting and physically fighting with each other.

I have certainly had clients where the father and the son ended up rolling around in the hallway of their home or in the family room fighting each other. One certainly does not want to have physical confrontations under such circumstances. Such only demonstrates that we have two "kids" fighting each other.

Corporal punishment has no place in coping with adolescents.

9. How do you know if your adolescent has a learning problem or "dyslexia"?

Dyslexia is the popular term seen on the local media and in the press. It actually means "difficulty with words" and, traditionally, has referred to difficulties with the written form of language or with words in print i.e. reading. There are various forms of Dyslexia including, for example, dysgraphia (problems with writing) and dyscalculia (problems with arithmetic).

More recently, the term Dyslexia has been expanded so that it is often used interchangeably with the term **Specific Learning Disorder (SLD)**. However, it is also true to say that most of the general population still know the condition as Dyslexia.

So, what is dyslexia or a SLD?

- The **disorder is in one or more of the individual's basic processes** such as auditory or visual memory, sequencing ability, visual-motor processing, or phonological awareness. In other words, the person has a problem taking in information through their ears (auditory) or eyes (visual), or he or she has a problem with logical sequencing and ordering, or the person has a problem with hand-eye coordination such that they are clumsy or have difficulty writing or finally, they experience difficulty distinguishing sounds and words (phonological awareness).

- The individual has **difficulty in learning**, specifically in relation to speaking, listening, reading, writing or mathematics.

- The disorder is **not primarily due to other causes** such as visual or hearing impairments, motor handicaps, mental retardation, emotional disturbances, or economic, environmental or cultural disadvantages. However, one or more of these can also occur along with learning disabilities.

- A **severe discrepancy** exists between the individual's **apparent potential for learning and their actual achievement levels in school**.

- It is to be noted that an individual with a specific learning disability still falls within the **normal intelligence** range; that is, they do not fall within the intellectually deficient or mentally deficient or retarded range.

It is also important to know that, statistically, around 10% of the population has a learning disorder of some kind. That is around 2-4 in every classroom.

Unfortunately, the sad fact is that many children and adolescents get missed and they continue to struggle academically with severe repercussions to their self-esteem and life generally.

How do you know if your teenager might have a learning problem?

The telltale "signs" are shown below, but it is important to stress that it is unlikely that an individual would exhibit all of them:

- difficulties in attending, e.g. short concentration span, easily distracted, daydreaming, not following instructions, not "listening"
- poor motor abilities, perhaps clumsy, poor fine motor coordination, poor or untidy or messy handwriting, slow in writing or copying things down

- perceptual and information-processing problems
- delayed speech or difficulty with language
- difficulties with written expression, misses deadlines for essays or assignments, only writes the bare minimum, avoids written work
- behind others or the class in reading, spelling or mathematics
- inappropriate social behavior, perhaps poor peer relationships, disruptive in class, class clown, annoys others
- poor organizational skills, loses pens, pencils and books, does not have the right books for the right lessons, leaves books, gym clothes and so on at home

What do you do if you think that your adolescent has a learning problem of some kind?

The only way of verifying a genuine learning problem is to consult with a psychologist and one who specializes in educational psychology; not just any psychologist will do. Ask the psychologist if he or she is a member of their professional association (e.g. Australian Psychological Society, American Psychological Association, British Psychological Society) and within the association itself, whether he or she has specialist expertise in learning disorders (e.g. being a member of the College of Educational and Developmental Psychologists).

Take your adolescent, if he or she is willing and if not, go along yourself with school reports and any other reports that might be available e.g. occasionally, there might a report from an occupational therapist or speech therapist or a school guidance officer. Discuss the situation and what reasons you might have for believing that your teenager might have a learning problem.

Most importantly though, the only way to confirm whether or not a learning difficulty is present is for the psychologist to undertake what is called an **"Intellectual & Educational Assessment"** where typically, the psychologist administers an intelligence test called the WISC along with a range of educational tests to assess if the adolescent is behind at all in areas such as reading, spelling and arithmetic.

After explaining the results, the psychologist should then write a full report with recommendations and strategies about how to cope with the learning problem if one exists.   For example, for an adolescent with a genuine Specific Learning Disorder i.e. Dyslexia, extra time can be allowed in timed tests and exams or if the adolescent has a writing problem, the use of a laptop in class and exams can be recommended.

Above all, if you are unsure, then seek to have your adolescent tested.

One of the sadnesses of being a psychologist is to test students in later years of schooling such as Grade 10, 11 or 12 only to find that the adolescent has had dyslexia which has gone undetected for all of his or her school life.

How is it that the school has not mentioned it or recommended a psychometric assessment? How these students have hung in there too, for all of their schooling is sometimes beyond me. How have they managed to stick at it day after day when each day is a failure experience where they are struggling and not coping?

It can only be that such students have very supportive parents and family, and perhaps personally are somewhat resilient and persistent. These students are a credit to themselves and their families.

Nevertheless, it is abysmal and a blight on our education systems that such students are not picked up earlier and that remedial help is not given at least by the mid primary school years.

10. How do you know if your child or adolescent has ADD or ADHD?

The popular press used to call it "**Hyperactivity**."

Actually, hyperactivity was the most widely studied disorder of childhood during the 1970s and 80s. Despite recent interest in ADD, however, the general notion of hyperactivity has been around for centuries.

More recently, the labels Attention Deficit Disorder (ADD) and more particularly, Attention Deficit Hyperactivity Disorder (ADHD) have been used. It is thought that the term ADD or ADHD is more appropriate since it highlights the general agreement that the *major problem in hyperactive children is one of paying attention, listening and concentrating.*

Interestingly, I heard from a colleague recently that ADD really stood for "Absent Discipline Disorder!" Certainly, there would be a number of professionals who would agree, that many times, poor parenting has really been the cause of poor behavior in children rather than the actual disorder ADD.

Regardless, definition and classification of ADHD has been a controversial question for some years. Despite decades of research, there is no single foolproof test, nor consensus on what classifies ADHD.

Part of the confusion comes from the fact that outwardly, ADHD children look apparently normal. Although the existence of ADHD seems to be agreed upon by clinicians and researchers, there is no uniformly acceptable definition of the disorder.

If, then, the criteria are so diverse, what symptoms are available to help in the diagnosis of ADHD?

Basically, **ADHD has been defined in the following ways**:

1) Behavioral problems, e.g. impulsivity, over-activity, inconsistency, disorganization, clumsiness, poor self-esteem, language deficits and specific learning disabilities;

2) An inability to stop, look and listen, i.e. to maintain attention and concentrate;

3) Frequent failure to follow verbal requests or instructions; does not seem to listen.

Possibly, the most common source of reference for diagnosis by psychologists and psychiatrists is the *"Diagnostic and Statistical Manual of Mental Disorders."* This states that the essential features of ADHD are signs of developmentally inappropriate attention, impulsivity, and hyperactivity.

How common is ADHD?

Researchers and clinicians agree that the incidence of the disorder is in the range of 1% - 5% of children.

While differences in the definitions used by professionals have an effect on the number of reported cases, it also appears that socio-economic status (SES) influences the likelihood of the complaint as a result of poorer pre-post natal medical care and nutrition; greater likelihood of family instability; and less education and information on child development and parent management techniques. In addition, ADD-H is a male-dominated complaint and as such, rates of ADHD vary between the sexes.

What causes ADHD?

The causes of ADHD are again debatable -- there are widely varying opinions and arguments. Some of the factors thought to be associated with ADHD include the following:

- difficulties in central auditory processing
- cognitive weaknesses including using one's thoughts to both focus and maintain attention and effort during problem solving
- minimal brain dysfunction as evidenced by motor in-coordination and mildly abnormal reflexes
- minor physical abnormalities
- genetic factors
- dietary considerations including food additives and refined sugars
- birth complications
- chaotic home environments and psychiatric disturbance in the parents
- difficult infant temperament especially in conjunction with poor parenting

It is clear that no single factor can adequately account for the symptoms of ADHD. In fact, it is probable that there are multiple factors causing the complaint.

What are the developmental stages of the disorder?

In sequence, taking the stages of the developmental course of hyperactive children, the following patterns are often recognized:

0-2 years: 1) not all hyperactive children show difficulties during this period, but a majority do.

2) problems are associated with temperament including eating, fussy and irregular eaters; sleeping, disturbances in sleep patterns including shorter periods of sleep; and activity level, restlessness, difficult to hold and restrain in cribs.

2-3 years: 1) those who were not difficult as infants now begin to show problems.

2) problems include non-compliance, restlessness, clumsiness and being accident prone, difficulties in taking naps or playing alone without parent attention, difficulties in toilet training.

3) parents may dismiss this period as the "terrible 2's" or transitory especially if it is the first child.

3-5 years: 1) during this phase, the parents often seek psychological help because the kindergarten or school staff also indicate that there are problems.

2) problems include non-compliance especially in public, poor peer interactions (i.e. aggression toward other children, selfishness with own possessions, demands other's possessions), destructive (i.e. due to clumsiness as well as anger), parents believe their child has less of a conscience than other children, child does

not seem to be responsive to ordinary disciplinary methods, and if disciplined may become very angry; child blames others for problems, parents have difficulty finding baby-sitters and may decrease socialization with friends and other families, possibly resulting in parental depression.

5 years and older:

1) problems at school with behavior and general performance emerge. School staff complain; decisions have to be made about keeping the child down in kindergarten because of "immaturity" or not being "school ready." Appearance of learning problems becomes highly probable, and they are not liked by other children and may become "loners" because of aggression, selfishness and clumsiness; continue to blame others for their problems, lying and petty theft may arise.

Later childhood:

1) problems continue with failure at school (i.e. bragging, lying, cheating, truancy as a way of gaining success or acceptance) and stress at home (i.e. arguments, tensions), and the child may also show depression and low self-esteem. Acting out behavior may increase due to frustration and chronic failure, and first contact with the law for minor offences such as trespass and verbal abuse may occur.

Does the disorder continue into adolescence and adulthood?

A number of myths exist about children outgrowing their complaints and catching up at puberty. In short, the disorder does persist into adolescence and adulthood, but not in every case. The symptoms have been found to continue into **adolescence** in about 50-80% of individuals.

In addition there are continued problems with poor academic performance, low self-image, and difficulties with peer relationships.

Associated antisocial behaviors also continue into adolescence in an average of 25% of cases. Alcohol abuse for example, and possible substance abuse, become obvious for this group.

In **adulthood**, the problems of adolescence seem to ease somewhat, partly as a result of the greater freedom given to adults. They still continue however to be impulsive, inattentive, and more restless than others.

It is not yet known however, whether hyperactive children as adults are more likely to have hyperactive children than are adults with a normal background and development.

"The average teenager still has all the faults that his parents outgrew."

(Author Unknown)

Treatment: What works?

Although ADHD cannot be cured, there are a number of treatment approaches that seem to have some success with ADHD children, such as drug management, behavior management, and cognitive or "thinking" therapy.

While not all children take medication for the disorder, **drug management** is thought to help 60%-70% of children who are **properly diagnosed** as hyperactive. However, it is also true that such drugs (e.g. Ritalin) have been heavily over-prescribed with parents often wanting a "quick fix."

When it is effective though, behavioral improvement is almost immediate, but no-one can predict how long the medication will be needed. Drug treatment is less effective for children under 5 years of age and is generally not prescribed after the age of 16.

Drug treatment has its primary effect only on attention span, memory and impulse control (i.e. it stimulates the concentration and attending centre of the brain), and although behavioral changes occur, medication has little effect on the improvement of academic achievement.

However, it has been suggested that there are critical side effects of some of the drugs such as stunting physical growth. Hence, parents need to carefully consider this whole issue of applying drugs for ADHD.

While drug treatment seems to assist in day to day management, other treatments are also required not only to assist academic performance, but also long-term social adjustment and self-esteem.

Behavior management programs are used in order for parents to obtain management strategies to handle their children. ADHD children seem to respond well to the structure and limits of such techniques, where the rules are explicit, and the consequences of appropriate and inappropriate behavior are given immediately.

Cognitive or "thinking" therapy focuses on children's "self-talk" as a way of teaching self-control. Children are taught strategies to stop and define the problem, consider several possible solutions before acting, monitor their own performance, and give themselves a pat on the back.

Nutritional supplements have more recently been suggested as assisting ADHD as well. There seems to be an increasing body of research suggesting that nutritional supplements are having positive effects for children with attention and concentration difficulties. The results on this though are not yet certain and parents need to proceed with some caution.

In summary, a variety of factors working together are likely to be the causes of ADHD.

Major symptoms include:
- poor attention and short-term memory;
- distractibility;
- impulsive and silly behavior which is sometimes dangerous to self and others;
- poor self-esteem and other emotional and psychological reactions.

Treatment and control of the disorder is effective in the majority of cases, with the use of drug treatment combined with behavior management and cognitive therapy.

11. What do you do about the school bully who picks on my teenager?

Surveys of 38,000 students in Australia for example, over a number of years by Dr Ken Rigby and a colleague of mine, Dr Phillip Slee, indicate that 15% of children said they were bullied weekly.

"He bullied, soothed and cajoled. In fact, he's awfully good at what he does, but how one wishes that he didn't work quite so hard doing it."

(John Corry; 1666-1726, Irish Politician)

Other studies from a number of countries e.g. Norway, England, United States, Japan, Ireland, Netherlands, have shown similar findings. Research also shows that the peak in bullying tends to occur in the younger grades (e.g. Grade 2) where 17% of students reported being bullied while in Grade 9 the percentages decreased to 3% of girls and 6.5% of boys.

A special note about a new trend in the last few years called "**Cyber-bullying**." This is the use of cell phones or mobile phones to send texts to a victim. It can also be played out via MSN or other chat websites on the internet. It is lethal because it is usually ongoing. In other words, you can't get away from it! It's just not restricted to school.

Many teenagers however, will not let on that they are being bullied either at school or over the internet. Adolescents may not want to say that they are being bullied because:

1) they don't want to look or sound weak or "pathetic",
2) they don't want the parents to go to the school and somehow embarrass them,
3) they don't want the teachers to know that they can't handle it,
4) they are afraid of any further retributions if the bully finds out,
5) they don't want to be seen as a "dobber" getting others into trouble.

Although the adolescent may **not** tell you initially that he or she is being bullied, typically, there are some signs such as the following:

- becoming short-tempered, intolerant, with perhaps some outbursts
- becoming teary, withdrawn or depressed
- obvious panic or anxiety about going to school
- a drop off in grades or a hint of school refusal
- asking for extra pocket money or maybe stealing (to buy off the bully or placate the bully somehow)
- continual stomach "upsets" or headaches that means that they need to stay home or frequent visits to the school sick room or being sent home because they are unwell
- wanting the parent to drop them off at the school gate rather than take the bus or walk or ride a bike
- trouble sleeping at night and awakening often through the night or difficulty dropping off to sleep

Clearly, the bullying has to stop. The impact on self-esteem can be very severe and damaging – at times, permanent.

The adolescent has to face it with strong support from

his or her family and school. If the issue is raised at home, in whatever form, then the parents must do all they can to support and encourage their offspring. The issue has to be raised at school and to this end, the parent has to find a compassionate, caring teacher who knows what to do.

Definitely, there should be no exposure of the victim. I have had well-intentioned teachers who have thought that they were doing the right thing by mediating and bringing both bully and victim together. It has then been then left up to me to try to redeem the situation where the bully's power has now increased as he knows that his victim has been worried, anxious and scared, and the victim is now also terrified!

If the supportive teacher, counselor or school chaplain can be found, then, the story of the bullying needs to be told in confidence. The bully needs to be brought in for a serious discussion and the parents or family of the bully involved. If the bullying continues, then the bully ought to be removed from the school. If the bullying involves threats of harm or injury) "We know where you live," "We're coming to get you," "Watch your back"), then call the police. Threats of this nature are an offense.

If help is not forthcoming from the school, the adolescent who is being victimized needs to leave and find another school to attend.

12. What do you do about girls at school who try a power play by deliberately excluding my daughter from the group?

In a sense, this kind of ostracism is also a form of bullying. Typically, in my experience, the girls are more subtle about their bullying and will do so in the form of gossip, teasing, and being one-up in relation to who is wearing the designer clothes, who went on the most exotic or expensive holiday over the Easter period as well as excluding others from the group.

In a sense, this is emotional or psychological bullying and can often be more damaging and more destructive than the physical bullying such as hitting, pushing, bumping that occurs.

In short, it is important to give the victim some skills to cope with the other more powerful girls. For example, if they tease or exclude or play the "I'm better than you" game, then the adolescent has two strategies that she could implement.

For example, see the flow chart below on the next page. Of course, it needs to be said quite plainly that to the very first put-down by the bully (e.g. "You're fat!"), the victim could also respond and come back with something that is slightly aggressive such as "Yeah right!" or "Stuff Off!" (or words to that effect).

The bully picks on the most vulnerable or the 'weakest' and if by some chance, the victim can muster enough courage to tell the bully where to get off when he or she is *first* picked on, this is usually sufficient to mean that the bully will go and find another culprit elsewhere.

"Bullies are always cowards at heart and may be credited with a pretty safe instinct in scenting their prey."

(Anna Julia Cooper; 1858-1964, US
Teacher & Writer)

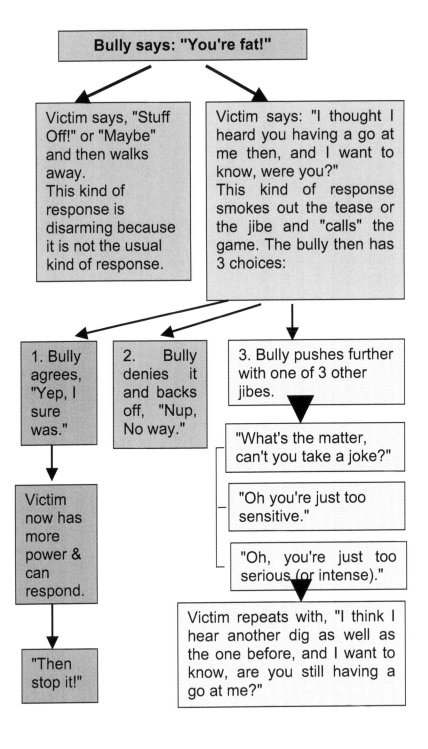

13. How do we handle grief or trauma in our teenager's life?

More and more teenagers seem to be confronted with trauma of some kind.

Maybe this has always been the case, but it hasn't been recognized or identified as much as it is now. Maybe it is the stresses of living in the new millennium that are also causing more trauma and crises than previously.

For example, adolescents have sought help clinically because one of their friends or peers has suicided or a friend has been killed in a motor vehicle accident or they were caught up in a robbery in a hotel or gas station or local store or caught up in a bomb threat or been involved in a car accident themselves.

Perhaps the trauma has not been as severe, but there is also certainly an impact with events such as parents divorcing or moving house or changing schools or losing a pet.

With trauma, the best advice is to seek professional help with a psychologist or psychiatrist.

Detailed below however, is the *sequence of events* that occur from a trauma situation (whatever that might be) through to the eventual working it through or laying it to rest.

It is important to try to understand what your adolescent has gone through.

```
┌─────────────────────────────┐
│  TRAUMA SITUATION OCCURS     │
└─────────────────────────────┘
```

Shock   i.e. Going white in the face, dizziness, nausea, increased heart rate, breathing becomes fast or shallow.

Disbelief   i.e. *"Is this really real?"*
"Is this really happening?"

Realization i.e. *"Yes, this is real, this is not my imagination; this is not a joke."*

Survival   i.e. *"What do I do to survive this?"* Sometimes a person's emotions become very flat, or they "freeze" or become very calm; sometimes people behave in ways that they later regret, but all their feelings and behaviors are oriented to doing **anything** to help them survive.

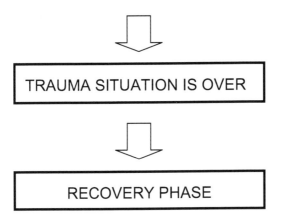

TRAUMA SITUATION IS OVER

RECOVERY PHASE

Generally, in the Recovery Phase, the symptoms from a trauma vary for individual people. They typically last only a short period of time (e.g. 1 - 2 months), but may last for much longer.

Recognizing that everyone goes through a difficult

time after a trauma and acknowledging that there are some common reactions helps people to feel less "unusual," less "crazy" and less isolated or alone. This is especially so for teenagers who need to know that it's "normal" to go through a series of "weird" emotions.

There are some **common emotions**, as listed below, which tend to occur **immediately** following a trauma. (Of course, not everyone experiences all of these emotions, but most experience some of them. Together with these feelings, people usually experience various physical or medical symptoms as well as behavioral reactions):

1. Shock
A feeling of disbelief –
"I can't believe it happened"
"It all happened so quickly"
"It all seems like a nightmare"

2. Guilt
A feeling of remorse at your feelings, thoughts or actions during a trauma –
"Maybe I could have prevented it"
"Maybe I'm to blame"
"I could have helped some of the people, but I didn't"
"I should have been more considerate"
"I should have acted differently"
"I shouldn't have been so selfish"
"I got out of it, but others didn't"

3. Anger
A sense of injustice or unfairness about it all –
"Why me?"
"Why at this particular time?"
"I really didn't need this now"
"Why didn't they take precautions?"

"Why weren't they more careful?"
"It's all so senseless"

4. Thought Difficulties
Lack of control over your thought processes –
"My mind is just racing, it won't turn off"
"All these thoughts keep racing into my mind"
"I get these strange thoughts now"
"I keep on reliving it and thinking about it"
"I don't trust people any longer"
"I'm suspicious of people now"
"I keep on getting flashbacks of the event"

5. Anxiety
A sense of tenseness and general anxiety –
"I feel trembly"
"I get panicky now whenever I . . ."
"I am afraid now to . . ."
"I take extra precautions now"
"I'm uptight"
"I feel insecure and vulnerable"

6. Depression
A sense of feeling low, isolated, cut-off, not supported and not in control –
"I feel so alone"
"I can't seem to get on top of this"
"I feel kind of remote and lost"
"I don't feel normal any longer"
"Will I ever get better?"

7. Reflection on Life
A realization that none of us has a monopoly on life and that, ultimately, death comes to each of us, and over that fact we have little control; a realization that perhaps our life priorities need changing or altering since trauma has a way of causing us to

refocus again on what is **really** important in life.

```
┌──────────────────────────────────────────┐
│              LAYING IT TO REST            │
└──────────────────────────────────────────┘
```

Working through the emotions above, the individual accepts that they are a little bit wiser now, the memories are still there and will remain, but it is now more in perspective.

It is this laying it to rest where professional help is advisable. Many people feel that they can handle it themselves especially macho adolescent males, but the reality is, that failure to adequately sort through the emotions can leave some "unfinished business" and ultimately possibly a Post-traumatic Stress Disorder (PTSD) which means that their crisis remains unresolved and at various times can rear itself and impact on people perhaps in unexpected ways.

Later common reactions might include:

- startled by loud noises
- suspicious of "shady" customers / clients / people / students
- distressed by television programs or news items showing robberies or trauma
- feeling paranoid
- fear of leaving home
- fear of the dark
- generally feeling insecure in public
- loss of confidence
- feeling of isolation
- not wanting to go to the place where the trauma occurred

However, you as a parent will certainly want to try to alleviate your adolescent's discomfort over **the initial hours or first few days** following a trauma situation.

Remember not to be an "*advice-giver"*, **it is more important to listen**. Listening is your most important gift to your teenager at this time. Listen to them and ask how he or she is feeling – "How do you feel?" "What are you thinking?" "What's going through your head?" "What's on your mind?"

When they give you a response simply paraphrase what they told you; don't evaluate it, judge it or in any way scrutinize it. Say something like,

- "So you're feeling kind of numb right now still coming to terms with what happened"
- "So you're wondering if in some way you could have prevented the accident from happening, is that it?"

Accepting what they are telling you helps them to understand that what they are going through is also acceptable.

If they do ask for guidance though, the following tips to them might be helpful:

- Within the first 24 – 48 hours, trying periods of strenuous physical exercise alternated with relaxation which will all help to alleviate some of the physical reactions
- Don't tippy-toe around them, but be prepared to give some concessions (e.g. prepare their favorite meal as a treat)
- Keep busy – structure their time – don't just allow them to sit around and think – they'll be "their own worst enemy"

- Assure them that they're normal and having natural reactions – don't let them label themselves as "crazy" – they haven't lost it!
- Allow them to talk to people – talk is the most healing medicine
- Be wary of numbing the pain with overuse of drugs or perhaps alcohol; we don't need to complicate this with a substance abuse problem!
- Tell them to reach out – people do care
- Keep their life as normal as possible
- Allow them to spend time with others
- Give them permission to feel rotten by sharing feelings with others
- Suggest that they keep a journal and write their way through those sleepless hours or write it "out of their system" so to speak
- Allow them to realize that those around them are also under stress, including the parents
- Make sure that they eat good, well balanced meals
- Don't allow them to make any big life changes
- Allow the adolescent to make as many daily decisions as possible which will give him or her a feeling of control over their life, i.e. if someone asks him or her what they want to eat – get them to answer even if he or she is not sure!

For further information on dealing with trauma with adolescents see the following web sites:

www.grieflink.asn.au
www.reachout.asn.au

14. What if you don't like their friends?

Sometimes we think that parental attempts to prevent adolescents from making their own choice of friends are often doomed to failure, because some of their relationships represent important emotional attachments.

Telling a teenager that he or she cannot associate with a particular person is probably a lost cause. Most teenagers leave for school early in the morning and do not return home until late afternoon. On weekends, they might be gone from home even longer. How can the parent ensure that the teenager is not, in fact, interacting with a non-preferred person?

Insisting that your adolescent comply with an unenforceable demand only sets up the teenager to lie and cheat on you. Certainly, the parent needs to explain (briefly, not a long lecture) why it is preferred that the teenager not keep company with a non-desirable person, but to insist on it when there is no way to enforce it is useless – and might even be harmful.

Nevertheless, as a parent, you can influence the situation somewhat by:

a. changing the adolescent's school if they are hanging around with the wrong group;

b. inviting particular adolescents to share your holidays with you whom you consider are reasonable young people and who are adolescents with whom you'd like your son or daughter to spend time;

c. sending your adolescent interstate or overseas to visit an uncle or cousin (or whoever) for the school holidays (or even a school term) in order to break the cycle of friends with whom they are associating.

15. When is the right time to do Career Guidance with my adolescent because I want to make sure that they have a goal and are motivated?

The most opportune time to begin career guidance in Australia at least, is midway through Year 10 (Sophomore year) when the student is aged around 15 -

16 years of age. In the USA for example, at the very least, Sophomore students in high school are meant to be preparing for the college application process. In the UK, this process for career focus occurs either at Year 10 or Year 11 (previously called the 4th or 5th Form).

"All children are artists. The problem is how to remain an artist once he grows up."

Pablo Picasso; 1881-1973, Spanish
Painter & Sculptor)

Education Departments have deemed that somewhere after mid-year (around about week 3 or 4 in Term 3), students need to select their subjects for Year 11 and their probable subjects for their final Year 12 (Grade 12). This can be a nerve wracking time and anxious for students and parents alike as well as for some teachers and coordinators.

Certainly, it needs to be said that one way of easing the stress is to undertake some career guidance so that students can focus more clearly on their subject choices, based on the bigger picture of where they might be headed in terms of a general career.

Any earlier than Year 10 (15 years) for career guidance is generally not appropriate because students seem to be too immature. Of course, it can be argued that Year 10 or the Sophomore year seems to be too early for selecting careers, but as I have said above, the requirement by the Departments of Education (and Independent or Private Schools) to choose subjects means that students need to at least consider in a general sense, where they might be headed in terms of a career path.

Certainly, there have been a number of parents who have repeatedly made comment that it was important for their son or daughter to have a career goal especially during that final graduation Year 12 when the going seems to get tough.

Having a goal assisted their motivation and gave a focus as to why they were putting themselves through this whole ordeal called Year 12 (i.e. Grade 12 or 6th Form).

Many independent, private schools and some public schools have an initial career guidance program at Year 10 level (10th Grade) where students undertake a Work Interests test such as the **Vocational Interest Questionnaire** (VIQ) authored by myself and Mr Garry Simcock who was previously from Prince Alfred College in South Australia. This test is now delivered to schools internationally via the Internet:

www.viq.com.au

It is also delivered to individuals at the following address where the person can immediately gain a profile of their work interests and see a list of jobs that are most suitable for them.

www.findacareerpath.com

A more comprehensive career guidance program however, is available through some private psychologists.

Make sure though that the psychologist is a member of their national associations such as the Australian, American or British Psychological Societies and within the Society or Association is a member of the College of Organizational Psychologists.

In my own psychology and coaching practice, we have a program that involves the following ***three-stage process***:

(a)   **An Initial Interview**. This is an important part of the guidance process, allowing us to meet the individual and essentially to get to know the person.   Each individual undertakes vocational guidance for specific reasons and we feel that it is important to have this information before testing occurs.

(b)   **Psychometric Testing**. The four areas of testing are outlined below. Testing takes around 1½ - 2 hours in total, and the teenager does the testing over the internet in their own time.

    i.   **Interests**
    Measures likes and dislikes in relation to work

    ii. **Values/Attitudes**
    Examines what motivates people to work

    iii. **Personality**
    Examines behavioral characteristics, personal strengths and work styles

    iv. **Work Style**
    Measures the way that a person works

(c)   **Counseling Session**. During this session, the results of the testing are discussed with the adolescent along with various career options and a **Career Action Plan** is devised. This session usually takes place 5-10 days following the testing session. The teenager leaves with a full report in hand.

If the career guidance is done over the internet or Skype rather than face to face, the report of course, is emailed prior to the final counseling session.

This kind of process is comprehensive in that it gives a good description of the individual's strengths and talents and based on this information, it is then possible to highlight the most appropriate or suitable jobs for that particular person.

As an aside, when I first began career guidance in the early 1970's, almost all my clients were adolescents, but now in this new millennium it is about 30% adolescents and 70% adults. The workplace is changing and adults too need to be aware of what their next career step might be or how they can best utilize their talents and resources.

16. Are "family conferences" a good idea?

Yes. Life in this century seems to becoming busier and busier, and with it, there seems to be less and less time for those around us.

Family members, for example, tend to become caught up in their own world with each going his or her own way. Probably this has always been the case, but in recent times, this trend seems to have increased.

Yet, the family is still the foundation of our society

where we learn to talk, to share, to grow and to learn who we are in interaction with others.

One way of ensuring that the family does make time to communicate is to organize what is called a *"family conference."* Of course, communications among family members is meant to happen informally and naturally, but the nature of 21st Century life now means that it may be important to program in special communication time.

A family conference is really nothing more than everyone in the family putting aside a specific time to talk together. They are usually held once per week. At the very least, they ought to be held whenever there is a change in the family "program" such as at the beginning of the school year or at the beginning of a new school term or when the parents start a new shift at work. Family conferences are sometimes scheduled on a regular night, or can be variable depending on the availability of family members.

What happens at a family conference? A number of approaches can be taken.

Families can take the opportunity to talk about how things are running generally. Are the family routines working well? What new routines need to be instituted or changed? Are there any grievances to be aired? What would you like to see this family do more of? What would you like to see this family do less of?

Families can also take the opportunity to "get to know each other" better.

For example, each family member can provide positive feedback about each other family member (e.g. What do I like best about each person? What are each member's strongest points? What is the nicest thing that each member has done for me?).

The family members take it in turn to receive this kind of feedback and the family moves systematically around the group giving their comments to individuals.

Sometimes, a variation on a theme can also mean that the family conference might organize a games night the following week. Board games, charades or any other kind of fun night is appropriate.

Family conferences? Sound strange? You will be surprised at how well they work and what you will learn about each other as well as how it strengthens family bonds.

17. What should I do about my daughter who goes on Facebook and My Space and puts up photos and information about herself on the internet and that now she says she has 239 "face book friends."

Join her! Make sure that you also join up with facebook and then you can monitor what she is putting up.

You don't have to put up too much personal information about yourself at all; it's really just an email and name. However, as a signed up member, you are then in a position to be able to check what your daughter is revealing and what others are saying to her.

Generally speaking, you wouldn't make specific comment to her about her content unless you felt it was inappropriate (and don't post any written comments on her Facebook site because that would naturally be embarrassing for her). She will know anyway that you are a "member" because you would be automatically notified that you were one of her "friends."

As the saying goes, "If you can't beat them, join them," but in this instance, it is not so much joining as it is monitoring.

18. What can I do about my 14-year-old adolescent daughter who wants at to go to a party where the parents are allowing alcohol and some of the teenagers are known to be binge drinking?

This is probably every parent's nightmare.

On the one hand the teen wants to be seen as "cool" and be with her friends at any party that is arranged, but on the other, the parents are horrified re the issue of safety and security for their daughter given the apparent mis-use of alcohol.

This sets the scene for a World War III argument. The adolescent argues that "It's not fair, all the other friends are allowed to go" and "You're just old fashioned and out of it" and "You just don't understand" and "All my friends will think that I'm a nerd if I don't go" (or words to that effect). The parents argue that they are worried (and usually worried sick) that "something might happen" and "It may not be you in the wrong, but others there who are drinking could be out of control" and that could be a major problem. What to do?

First, there is the talk with the adolescent. Remember that this is not a discussion as they're going out the door somewhere. It might be at night when they are in bed or even while they are "captive" in the car with you. It is a **calm** conversation. Revisit the Chapter 3 on *"Independence"* and review the sections on *"How do parents let go"* and *"How do you resolve conflict when it occurs."* If after a calm discussion of the whole issue, you cannot let your daughter go to the party, you might want to try and work out what else she could do rather than just stay home and brood about the good time that she thinks that she's missing.

Second, contact the parents who are having the party and check that alcohol is being allowed. If this embarrasses your daughter, then simply, that's too bad. After-all, you are the parent. If alcohol is being permitted, you might say something to the other parents like you have a problem with that given the binge drinking that is occurring with adolescents and that you will now have to re-consider your options (without saying what those options are). By the way, if you happen to know the other parents of your daughter's friends, then give them a call and chances are you'll find that most of them are as worried as you might be (if they're not, they ought to be!). If you find that other parents are also very concerned, then maybe you can arrange for a group of your daughter's friends to have an alternative party. You're not against parties, just those that spell disaster in some way.

If you decide, for whatever reasons, that your daughter is to go to the party, part of the contract about attending would be for you to drop her off and pick her up and for her to be open and honest with you about what actually did happen at the party (without you saying "I told you so" or similar.

Finally, if she does attend, reassure her that you love her and that you trust her.

CHAPTER 7 SUMMARY

What are some of the most common questions that I have been asked?

1. **What do you do in a situation where a teenager who is obviously upset, refuses to communicate, but is quite rude in their mannerisms and responses to our advances as parents?**

2. **Should adolescents receive pocket money and if so, how much is enough?**

3. **How do you know if your teenager is on drugs?**

4. **What can you do about the influence of the peer group because the adolescent's friends seem to have more sway over the adolescent than their parents do?**

5. **How do you make adolescents responsible?**

6. **How do you make teenagers do their chores?**

7. **Should a teenager be punished and if so, what is appropriate?**

8. **Should we smack or spank our kids?**

9. **How do you know if your adolescent has a learning problem or "dyslexia?"**

10. **How do you know if your child or adolescent has ADD or ADHD?**

11. What do you do about the school bully who picks on my teenager?

12. What do you do about girls at school who try a power play by deliberately excluding my daughter from the group?

13. How do we handle grief or trauma in our teenager's life?

14. What if you don't like their friends?

15. When is the right time to do Career Guidance with my teenager because I want to make sure that they have a goal and are motivated?

16. Are "family conferences" a good idea?

17. What should I do about my daughter who goes on Facebook and My Space and puts up photos and information about herself on the internet and that now she says she has 239 "face book friends?"

18. What can I do about my 14-year-old adolescent daughter who wants at to go to a party where the parents are allowing alcohol and some of the teenagers are known to be binge drinking?

CHAPTER 8

Epilogue

Finally, parenting along with being a marriage partner or permanent partner is one of the most difficult roles that I know. Both roles come with **no** real training or instruction. We "fly by the seat of our pants".

Somehow or other, we get it more or less right. Naturally, in hindsight we can often see where we could have done it differently, but then of course, that's the distinct advantage of hindsight. Nevertheless, we gave it our best shot. Our children could ask for nothing more.

A final story. A story about eagles; those majestic birds. It is not my story, it's from David McNally, (*"Even Eagles Need a Push,"* 1990), but one that is relevant here.

> *The eagle gently coaxed her offspring toward the edge of the nest. Her heart quivered with conflicting emotions as she felt their resistance to her persistent nudging. "Why does the thrill of soaring have to begin with the fear of falling?" she thought. This ageless question was still unanswered for her.*

As in the tradition of the species, her nest was located high on the shelf of a sheer rock face. Below there was nothing but air to support the wings of each child. "Is it possible that this time it will not work?" she thought. Despite her fears, the eagle knew it was time. Her parental mission was all but complete. There remained one final task – the push.

The eagle drew courage from an innate wisdom. Until her children discovered their wings, there was no purpose for their lives. Until they learned how to soar, they would fail to understand the privilege it wants to have been born an eagle. The push was the greatest gift that she had to offer. It was her supreme act of love.

And so, one by one, she pushed them, and they flew!

That is the parental role in adolescence.

Between **Mr and Mrs Smith and Joanne Smith.**

Mother and father would like Joanne to:

1. let them know about her movements when she goes out at night by discussing well beforehand where she is going and with whom:
   letting them know by SMS if she moves from one place to another when she's out
   letting them know when she'll be home;
2. be less moody; she won't go silent ('sulk') for hours on end when reprimanded or thwarted and instead, will remain pleasant and courteous;
3. be more ready to say sorry; i.e. she will apologize when she's been in the wrong;
4. be more motivated regarding her school work (e.g. homework); i.e. she will put in at least an hour per night;
5. stop being so rude to her father, i.e. walking out when he gives her advice;
6. keep her room tidy such that there are no clothes or things left on the floor at any time.

Joanne would like her mother and father to:

1. stop criticizing her friends all the time; i.e. stop calling them names and saying they're no good, unless they are making a particular, constructive comment;
2. admit when they are in the wrong, i.e. they will apologize when they have been in the wrong in their discussions with her;
3. listen to her when she has a point of view to express; i.e. understand her perspective and be able to express that perspective back to her;

4. give her more pocket money (a sum agreed) and to review the amount every six months in the light of the rising expense and changing nature of her commitments.

All agree

1. that the terms of the contract will not be changed except by mutual discussion and agreement;
2. that disputes will be settled by the witness (grandmother), whom all accept to be objective and fair-minded;
3. that successful execution of the contract for a month will be rewarded by an agreed family treat (first month: an outing to a posh (named) restaurant);
4. that failure to carry out individual terms of the contract will result in a fine on each occasion: an amount of X for Joanne; and Y amount for Mr and Mrs Smith respectively. The money is to go in a 'penalty box' (kept by the grandmother), the proceeds of which will go to a charity of her choice.

Signed   Joanne ....

        Mr Smith ....

        Mrs Smith ....

        Grandmother (witness) ....…..

ABOUT THE AUTHOR

CROSSWAYS COACHING

Dr DARRYL G CROSS
PhD (Psychology)

Psychologist
& Coach

Fellow, Australian Psychological Society
Fellow, Australian Institute of Management
Certified Personal & Executive Coach, College of Exec Coaching
Professional Certified Coach, International Coach Federation
Member, National Speakers Association
Member, Family Business Australia
Accredited Facilitator, Mindshop Australia Ltd
Foreign Affiliate, American Psychological Association
Registered Psychologist

Dr Darryl Cross is both a **clinical and organizational psychologist** as well as personal and executive coach along with being an author, international speaker and university lecturer.

Importantly, Darryl has successfully raised three adolescents who are now all adults.

Professionally, he acted as an Honorary Consultant to the Catholic Family Welfare Bureau in Brisbane, Queensland for six years, was Director of a unit for children with severe behavioral disorders at the Women's & Children's Hospital in Adelaide for three years, and ran his own private psychology practice for 19 years.

Having gone through the discipline of tertiary study, he completed his Psychology Honours Degree in Psychology at Flinders University, South Australia. He gained his Doctorate in Psychology from the University of Queensland.

More recently, Darryl completed a Professional Development Certificate in Coaching Practice through the Department of Psychology at the University of Sydney, and then completed graduate studies in coaching with the College of Executive Coaching in California, USA. He is now a **Professional and Certified Coach** with the International Coach Federation.

He **knows how organizations work** from his first appointment for three years as an Occupational Psychologist with the Australian Federal Government and then when he subsequently tutored and lectured in Psychology at the University of Queensland in Brisbane for seven years and lectured at Macquarie University in Sydney, New South Wales for two years. He is currently a sessional lecturer at the University of South Australia.

Darryl Cross has been **speaking and training** for almost three decades on a variety of seminars for business, professional and non-professional groups. In terms of adolescents, he runs workshops or seminars to a variety of Parent & Friends Associations as well as teacher groups.

He has spoken internationally at numerous conferences and symposia and presented workshops in countries such as the United Kingdom, USA and South-East Asia.

As an **author**, Darryl has published numerous papers for national and overseas academic journals, as well as articles for the popular press and also written a book on Parenting 5-12 year old children and produced a Video-DVD on the same topic.

Go to **www.growingupchildren.com** for a download of the book on raising 5 – 12-year-olds plus a bonus report on the "17 Extra Hints on Raising Children".

He is heard regularly on talk-back radio and is often seen on various segments on television as well as in the print media. He knows what he's talking about and is called upon to give his opinion.

www.drdarryl.com
www.crossways.com.au
www.growingupchildren.com
www.teenagertroubleshooting.com

8468895R0

Made in the USA
Charleston, SC
12 June 2011